The Social Context of Teaching

Psychology and Education

General Editor: Gerald Cortis

The Social Context of Teaching

Gerald Cortis

Open Books
London

First published 1977 by Open Books Publishing Ltd
21 Tower Street, London WC2H 9NS

Hardback: ISBN 0 7291 0018 9

Paperback: ISBN 0 7291 0013 8

Filmset in 10pt Linotron Imprint

Printed by T. & A. Constable Ltd
Hopetoun Street, Edinburgh

Contents

Acknowledgements

I should like to acknowledge my debt to my colleagues at the University of Birmingham, both academic staff and students, for their many helpful suggestions, their constructive criticisms and, above all, their support. I am particularly grateful to my research students, Anne Grayson and Penny Barnett, who spent many hours alone and together with me considering the manuscript; to Marcia Rosen for her patience and devotion on the secretarial side; and to Peter Platt for his most generous assistance in the matter of library resources.

Editor's introduction

What actually happens in teaching? Outwardly most teaching consists of one person exchanging words and glances with a number of others interspersed with activities like reading, writing and practical work. Inwardly learning is assumed to follow. That it often does not forms the setting for this book. Teachers are not always the free agents they may suppose themselves to be, since they bring to their workplace, the classroom, not only their 'independent' psychological dispositions but also the social frameworks derived from the wider society in which they live. A teacher may choose to teach a subject more or less well, avoiding matter that he takes to be irrelevant, or matter he may not know intimately. A teacher often has no choice however about the teaching circumstances in which he finds himself. He has no choice in many cases of the pupils he teaches, the colleagues with whom he works or the administrative structures he encounters. So the book examines the effects of social groups and structures, the development of work roles and the performance of professional social skills, all of which extend our psychological vision of how the teacher operates in his day-to-day work.

The Social Context of Teaching is one of the titles in the *Psychology and Education* series. Though consumer preference does not constitute the sole criterion of selecting topics for course design, such a preference is a demand that both authors and publishers have not usually been able to meet with exactitude, since reliable information about demand has not been readily available until now. The selection of titles in this series was based on the results of an extensive nationwide survey of teachers of educational studies on the staffs of polytechnics and colleges that I carried out in 1973. The five titles represent the areas that teachers in higher education rated as the most essential elements in their actual or proposed courses in the psychological area of education. The authors, who have all had extensive teaching experience themselves, have taken as their principal aim the introduction of important psychological concepts in each area that are relevant to both educational theory and practice. Our purpose has been to write simply and clearly so that key areas are revealed and a framework is provided on which a student can build further knowledge. The framework embraces both new and long-standing concepts, since new knowledge has a relation to time past. The unity in the series arises from the ultimate selection of the five titles (in terms of the highest survey ratings) by the consumers themselves, though each title has been designed to stand on its own. Given the hybrid nature of both psychology and education some minor overlap of topic areas is inevitable and, in many ways, welcome.

References in the text to the work of other writers, e.g. Jones (1975) are provided so that students may be encouraged, where appropriate, to follow up the source named. The book or article so quoted will be listed in the References (which also double as a Name Index) at the back of the book.

Gerald Cortis

Preface

While I was in the final stages of writing this book, the BBC showed a documentary film entitled *The Human Conspiracy*, which, while not concerned with teaching as such, covered similar subject matter in the field of human behaviour.

In the book of the film Calder (1976) notes, 'People make people, not just by breeding them but by shaping one another's behaviour . . . [we] conspire to encourage proper behaviour and to check what is improper.' He suggests, in fact, that we are all conspirators from our earliest years, we indeed have to be to survive, and this conspiracy is governed by the nature of our social relations with each other. Calder concludes that 'the hallmark of human behaviour is etiquette rather than love'.

In general these sentiments were in accord with the approach I had already taken, for teachers above all 'make people', and are officially charged with doing so in a unique way. They adopt their own 'etiquette', yet this can only be effective in the conditions imposed on them by the nature both of schools and of the wider society in which they work, in fact within the *social context* of their job. In treating this theme, then, I have had at times to cross the boundaries between social psychology and sociology, for in many respects the areas complement each other. As a psychologist I hold that psychological experiences — for example, 'Why are men motivated to work?' — are *phenomena* in their own right. A sociologist might well say, however, that such psychological experiences *were derived from the social structure in which they occurred.* I take the former view while recognising that the latter has substance and relevance and needs to be considered in any account of teaching as a form of social behaviour.

The book begins by examining the nature of interaction in classroom groups, the development of group structure and the processes of norm formation. In the light of such perceptions it then looks at the way in which persons perceive each other and the type of communication that teaching entails.

We next examine the topic of leadership in teaching, the inevitable conflicts that arise from exercising it and their possible resolution. This is followed by a consideration of the problems of communication in teaching, the processes of social learning, and the practical issues of cooperation, competition, punishment and control.

Finally, we consider teacher behaviour in the organisational setting. The nature of organisational life, the motivation for working in organisations and the topic of organisational climate are discussed. The concluding section is devoted to an examination of the Hawthorne experiment and the implications for teaching arising from it.

The experiments described have been selected as examples of the processes that can operate, or actually do operate, in classrooms. However, like all selections they represent only a minor part of a much greater whole and need to be complemented by further reading.

1

Interaction in classroom groups

Introduction

Men live and work in groups, and the school class is one form of institutionalised group of which most of Western mankind will have had experience. There is no single clear-cut definition of a group that will serve on every occasion but essentially it resides in the dependence upon each other of two or more people in a relationship that each one perceives as having some recognisable unity. Members of a group form clear impressions of each other from meeting face to face, and from this knowledge *interaction* arises. *Interaction* means that each member reacts to the behaviour of each other member. Group members also have the quality of not only interacting with each other but of acting together as a unit towards the external environment.

The concept of the 'group' itself is a highly contentious one and Golembiewski (1962) discusses the problem of definition by comparing the view of a number of social scientists. He points out that the generic term 'group' is a useful one but that it is useful only within limits. The conflict is basically between (1) those who hold that a group's behaviour is the sum of the actions of the individuals who constitute it and (2) those who hold that the membership of the group itself imposes a 'collective mind' or 'group consciousness' as distinct from the minds of the individuals of whom the group is composed. This 'collective mind' itself can be considered as an entity in describing a group's behaviour.

DEFINITION OF A GROUP

This whole issue of group behaviour raises interesting questions as to the differences between individual and group action. A precise and unequivocal definition of a group is, as we have said, difficult to give. A convenient working definition for our purposes might be as follows:

1 A group is a set of persons among whom there exists a definable or observable set of relations. The word 'group', then, can refer not only to a set of persons but to the place where the interaction occurs (in our case, for example, we are concerned particularly with classrooms) and what happens there.

2 A group is a set of persons or systems that not only affect each other and depend on each other but respond to outside influences as well.

3 Put another way a group is composed first of a set of persons and second of a collection of interdependent persons.

4 A group generally has a goal. A goal may be defined as 'the collective pursuit of a particular end'.

5 Groups may be large or small. 'Small' groups may be technically defined as a set of persons numbering from two to about twenty, 'large' groups as any number above that. The boundary between 'small' and 'large' is arbitrary.

Group boundaries   The question of 'boundaries', however, is particularly important in defining group membership, those who are 'within' the boundary being members, those 'outside' the boundary not being members. In the school such problems of boundary definition are of course easier to comprehend because the classroom group is physically located for the major portion of its activity in one place. One is or one is not a member by virtue of this location factor, but even here the issues are not unequivocal, for if a pupil only attends school for 49 per cent of the time, being absent for the larger part, i.e. 51 per cent, is he or is he not a member? For all practical purposes we shall conclude that he is, for as far as school-age pupils are concerned the law defines and determines their status and their location fairly accurately.

Group characteristics All groups have certain general properties or characteristics in common, such as *communication, structure, cohesiveness, norms* and *goals.* Members *communicate* with each other in speech or writing. There is a *structure* within the group whereby members occupy different positions or 'roles'. One role may be more highly regarded than another either by members within the group or by outside observers, and one role may be of a different kind from another. The *cohesiveness* of a group is determined by how attractive members find each other and by how the tasks on which a group is engaged appeal to members. The more the task appeals the more likely are members to work together and stay together in pursuing it. Because the individual within a group is subject to pressures to conform to the expectations of others (and in turn, or perhaps simultaneously, imposes his own pressures on others) the group develops collective expectations or *norms of behaviour.* Groups have, as we have noted, a purpose or *goal* towards which their members strive. Even among informal groups who may be concerned only with purely social activity, members tend to act in a goal-oriented manner even if in achieving so simple a goal as when and where they are going to meet again.

The nature of the classroom group

Getzels and Thelen (1960) point out the distinctive nature of the classroom group, noting that its goal is learning, that such learning is 'technically' compulsory, and that members have no real control over the selection of its leader. In theory no appeal against his leadership is allowed. In real-life, however, some individual pupils behave so badly as to earn exclusion from the group. Hence they could be said to 'appeal' successfully against a particular teacher's leadership in that they are removed from his charge.

PRINCIPLES OF CLASSROOM WORK GROUP
Though the basic principles of classroom group action may be compared to those of other work groups, care is needed in

applying the broad principles of group psychology to the classroom. Each work group is different in nature and in structure from other work groups, though certain common dimensions apply to all. Technically the classroom is a *formal work group* and as such its members' functions are laid down (or *prescribed*) by those outside it — unlike *informal work groups* who will generate their own goals and objectives. The organisational structure of responsibilities and roles are formally prescribed too. Nevertheless the informal structure within a class group may still largely determine how it acts, and such informal structures are extremely powerful. Pupils, for example, may combine together to thwart or assist the teacher in the attainment of particular goals depending upon how they view such goals in the light of what they consider to be their own welfare.

As a formally organised work group the class group is established by an authority (in the case of Great Britain the local government authority) under the force of law and acting on behalf of the community to accomplish certain changes in the behaviours of those specifically committed to its charge. It is generally part of a larger organisation, the school, though in some cases it may be a unit of its own. An example of the latter would be the small units for pupils with behavioural problems or the one-class schools in rural areas that have existed for some years and which are in effect both a class and a school.

PRINCIPLES OF OTHER FORMAL WORK GROUPS

Other formal work groups are also established to accomplish certain changes in our society. Very often these changes are industrial processes concerned with changing raw materials into saleable products such as motor cars or television sets. In these groups the majority of the workforce is neither given nor generally seeks the task of determining how the product is to be shaped or made, or indeed what particular product is produced. There are exceptions, of course, and moves are being made to give industrial workers a greater say in their working practices, but generally, at the moment, their involvement is limited. The end product which constitutes the purpose of the group is determined before the group itself is organised.

In describing other formal work groups and their similarities to classroom groups it is relevant to point out an important dissimilarity. With changing social conditions class groups are tending more and more to the status of informal groups because they are demanding more say in how the 'product', i.e. *the learning experiences of each of the pupil members*, is to be shaped or constructed. Indeed some, perhaps a minority, are virtually determining what product is actually produced. This objective is sometimes attained, not by the positive step of joint discussions between leaders and led, that is between teachers and pupils, but by the non-cooperation of the pupils with the ends or goals and the methods or learning experiences that the teacher prescribes. It is important to emphasise that it is not always wilful non-cooperation either but can arise through the pupil's lack of perception of what teachers are really trying to do. Similarly it can also arise from the teacher's lack of perception of what pupils are capable of doing.

GROUP PRODUCTIVITY

The whole comparison between classroom groups and other formal work groups is rather hazardous because the techniques for measuring productivity are less reliable in the case of classrooms than of factory groups. At the end of a day, a week or a month it will be fairly easy to measure productivity in industrial settings by the number of cars or television sets or whatever that have been produced. There will be difficulties in that if only part of the factory is working, the other half being on strike, only parts of the finished article, e.g. the bodywork of a motor car, may have been produced by one group. In these it will be difficult to determine how many parts make the equivalent of one whole motor car. None the less the principle is clear whatever difficulties arise from actually counting the number of products made. This illustrates the point that industrial processes are more complex in their organisational layout because one group of workers will depend on another group in different ways from that of classroom groups which are more self-contained.

Given, then, that the accurate measurement of productivity is more easily applied to industrial and commercial settings than to classroom or school settings but that both are formal work groups, it can be seen that serious problems arise in assessing the latter's effectiveness. A formal work group, as a condition of its existence, should be able to point to the attainment of its goals, one of which might be the number of articles produced. But class groups are seldom able to do this in the same way, because the measuring devices available to educators will yield equivocal results. That is to say the measurement of any changes in pupil behaviour will be capable of many different interpretations, unlike the case of producing motor cars where a definite number can be quoted, can be seen and can be accepted as a real measure of productivity. How can a class group cite Johnny's improved social sense, Jenny's loss of timidity concerning number processes, Jan's mastery of irregular French verbs, as un-equivocal evidence of productivity? One method would be by some form of examination, preferably an examination whose standard had been set by trying it out on a large number of children of particular ages and working out standards or norms of performance for these ages. This is termed a standardised test. But even test results can be notoriously variable and difficult to interpret. What can we say of productivity if a pupil gets poorer results on a particular test a month after getting a better result? A popular measure of class group and school effectiveness or productivity at the sixteen-years-of-age level is the percentage number of O-level passes in the General Certificate of Education. But the fallibility of such a measure was clearly demonstrated for all to see some years ago. Certain heads of secondary schools entered the same candidates for two different GCE O-level examinations and reported the discrep-ant results — a candidate who 'failed' in one being 'passed' in the other, a candidate who 'passed at the bottom level' obtaining a 'high-level pass' in the other and so on.

The problem of using examinations — whether internally

administered, like a standardised test, or externally administered, like the GCE — as a class group's measure of productivity can be their effect upon the whole interactional and behavioural processes of the group. They can become ends in themselves. Indeed at the older age ranges of the secondary school they are often the dominating and principal influence on the curriculum. These effects are called 'backwash' effects. The 'backwash' effect can be illustrated by comparison with the industrial model. We make motor cars presumably to make our lives more comfortable, to enable us to save time by not walking, to transport our luggage and so on. Levels of productivity are taken incidentally to provide a measure of the producers' effectiveness in producing, for example, more motor cars this month than last month. In these days particularly, productivity is also measured in relation to the cost of the labour and the raw materials involved.

If the same model were applied to motor cars as is now often applied to class group and school processes, motor cars would not be produced for their ultimate benefits to mankind (if any) but to meet targets such as the number who were satisfactorily driven off the assembly line, the tightness of the nuts on various parts of the assembly, the satisfactory coverage of the bodywork with paint and so on. These industrial examination techniques are called 'quality-control procedures' and while important in themselves are subsidiary to the ultimate use and value of the product. They are not the sole end of the process. It would be absurd to use such procedures as a measure of whether or not class groups and schools are achieving their goals. That it is absurd does not stop some observers from using examination results (which are the school's form of 'quality control') for just that purpose. It is, however, the unique nature of the end process or product and the ways of achieving it that differentiate class groups from other formal work groups.

DIFFERENCES BETWEEN CLASS GROUPS AND OTHER WORK GROUPS

A class group differs then from other work groups in the

following three ways:

1 It has a different purpose from most work groups.

2 The methods necessary for it to achieve its goals are quite distinctive from those of other work groups.

3 Its membership is dissimilar from most other work groups. The uniqueness of the class group stems from the fact that it is organised to produce changes in its members themselves but the monitoring and assessment of any change, remains open to question. The goals of the group are externally prescribed and while here again such prescription is fairly vague and equivocal — 'to produce "good" citizens', 'to produce citizens who can function in a "free" society' — the nature of the group is unique in that its members not only create the product but are themselves the product. Because the class group is in theory organised to produce changes in the members themselves, it makes its tasks and activities rather unlike those of most other groups.

The class group by its nature is composed of members more similar than dissimilar to each other by virtue of their age, developmental levels and interests. It is much more homogeneous than other work groups whose composition is often quite a random matter as far as personal interests, age and so forth are concerned. In such other groups, members are only similar in regard to particular skills or knowledge which may even be developed 'on the job' and from the group pressures themselves.

The compulsory element in class-group membership has already been noted and it clearly distinguishes such working groups from other types. Members cannot normally leave class groups, and this produces its own type of group characteristics based upon the lack of choice that the participants have. In few other groups is such a compulsory element so evident as in the classroom group.

In its goals, its tasks and its compulsory membership lie the essential distinguishing marks of classroom groups as compared with other groups, and it is these particular areas that will exert a profound influence on their operation.

Theoretical considerations in studying classroom groups

In considering the theoretical considerations that underlie any attempt to explain the way groups think, act and have their being, Cartwright and Zander (1969) list eight principal approaches. However, they are at pains to point out that any one is not exclusive of any other and that in studying group activity an investigator might use several simultaneously. These approaches revolve around both individual and group dimensions and pose, say the authors, four important questions:

1 What is the proper relation between data collection and theory building?

2 What are the proper objects of study and techniques of observation?

3 What are the basic variables that determine what happens in groups?

4 How can the many factors affecting group life be combined into a comprehensive conceptual system?

(Perhaps we should briefly define here the meanings of the words *data* and *variable*, words which occur throughout accounts of research. *Data* are figures, ratings, check-lists and other information collected in experiments, surveys and descriptive studies. *Variables* are attributes or qualities which exhibit differences in amount and which vary along some dimension, e.g. scores on standardised tests of attainment.)

RESEARCH AND CONCEPTUAL ISSUES

The situation posed by Cartwright and Zander above is a good illustration in miniature of some of the problems of psychological research at large. Do we construct or do we have handed down to us theories of group behaviour which we then investigate in terms of the data we collect about individuals in groups? Alternatively do we do it the other way round, namely, collect data about group activity and construct theories on the basis of what we have observed? Perhaps in all sciences, and not least in the human ones, we need to do both. As I have said elsewhere (Cortis 1973):

> So in all sciences we have a continuous process of observation, the erection of hypotheses, proof or disproof, more observation, more hypothesis and so on. No final certainty or absolute truth reigns in the natural sciences. A theory is tenable only for the moment. When further facts are discovered we may modify a theory or abandon it for another which in turn will, perhaps at some very distant point in the future, undergo the same process of abandonment or modification.

Hence in this book we shall discuss theories that have been or can be tested, and theories that have not been tested, but which are perhaps moving towards the testable stage. In some cases, however, the ideas are likely to be in the realm of conjecture, only worth posing as being likely to produce the basis of sound theory.

Is the proper object of study, then, small groups, large groups, individuals or combinations of all three? How do we observe their behaviour and what influence does the observer have on the processes of the group? Do we write down our observations of the group perhaps at some time interval, do we telerecord or do we film? Are the basic variables that determine what happens in the group its size, or the environment in which it operates, or the psychosocial tendencies of the individuals concerned, or all three?

There is a whole host of questions raised here which in turn give rise to many more. These make the emergence of a comprehensive conceptual system very difficult to imagine and, the area being one in which many different disciplines are engaged (e.g. social psychologists, sociologists, psychoanalysts, ethologists), there is also confusion about the technical terms that are used. As Cartwright and Zander (1969) say:

> The development of any science seems to work progressively toward a satisfactory answer to the question of how data collection and theory building should be related. It appears

that all the sciences have stemmed initially from armchair speculation; most can be traced back to a definite tradition in philosophy. For each developed science it can be said that at some point in history some people became dissatisfied with speculation and undertook to observe carefully and objectively the phenomena in question. Often the rebellion against speculation created an extreme position that ignored theory and let the data 'speak for themselves'. Finally, as a branch of science became more mature, theory building and data collection assumed a more interdependent relation to each other. In its advanced stage the scientific enterprise consists of developing hypotheses and theories from observations, checking these theoretical formulations by new observations and experiments, revising the hypotheses, checking these new hypotheses in new investigations and so on, over and over again. In the process, more and more comprehensive theoretical systems emerge, each part of which has a firm empirical basis.

In general, then, much of the current research in group dynamics is concerned with the relation of variables such as how group size is related to the expression of group opinion, and how members' preference for acting as a group modifies, changes or completely alters their sentiments towards an outside object or state. Again no comprehensive theoretical framework has emerged from the mass of material published but one promising line was the attempt by March and Simon (1958) to develop schemata or 'maps' to show how different investigators' conclusions may be combined to produce a meaningful picture of how one set of terms is related to another.

In the educational context, as far as group processes go, the picture is not too discouraging. While each classroom is somewhat different from every other, in some ways much similarity exists and it is possible in many cases to generalise findings more widely. It is possible to be somewhat more confident about the applicability of findings across a wider range when, for example, one is not in the position of having to compare such extremes as Chinese waiters in San Francisco and factory operatives in Bradford. None the less much of the evidence is fragmentary and rudimentary at least in Britain. This arises, I would suggest, for two reasons. First, the area of social psychology generally is still struggling for a wider recognition in the hierarchy of the social sciences. Second, there is a good deal of resistance to research in general, and research into groups in particular, in many kinds of schools on 'invasion of privacy' grounds.

The social structure of classroom groups

Morrison and McIntyre (1973) describe the nature of the structure of the classroom group thus:

> Among the pupils in every classroom, there are more or less stable patterns of interaction. The class may or may not be divided into several sub-groups; if there are such sub-groups, they may be hostile, friendly or tolerant towards one another; each member of the class may communicate with most others, only with those in his own sub-group, predominantly with one or two high-status members of the class, or very rarely with anyone. The nature of the class structure has important bearings on the type of relationships which it is possible for a teacher to establish with his pupils, and on the problems with which he is likely to be faced.

It is important to realise that in talking of the classroom group it is not merely a descriptive term to be applied solely to the actual assemblage of teacher and pupils within four walls which is called a classroom. One aspect of the structure is certainly described in this fashion but such a group can break down into smaller groups. These will in turn combine, compete, break up and reform in varying ways during the course of any fixed period of time. Hence the teacher is an overseer to a number of groups when he is technically only the class teacher for one class. The question of what exactly constitutes 'a group' as distinct from an aggregate or crowd is of course an important one and a number of school classes might be considered a little large to be labelled groups. 'Children', suggests Veness (1962), 'do not interact freely in groups larger than about thirty.' But it seems appropriate to use the term 'classroom group' of those pupils who function under one teacher, even if they be slightly over the 'magic' number since, as I have suggested, such a collection of pupils is only static and perceived as a while for very short periods indeed.

TYPES OF GROUPS

1 *The dyad.* The simplest type of group (called a *dyad*) consists of two persons and is an example of the most uncomplicated piece of social interaction. Much behaviour of a more diffuse and complicated nature can be explained by reference to this group. Like all groups, this example of interaction is a distinct entity which possesses characteristics and properties that can be observed, measured, classified and predicted.

Newcomb's experiment Newcomb (1961) has illustrated experimentally the growth in stability of one person's attraction for another following prolonged contact between them. Two groups of seventeen male students, who were total strangers to each other, served as subjects in successive years. They lived and took their meals together in a house reserved to them for a period of sixteen weeks. Every week they completed a set of questionnaires, attitude scales and other psychological tests, many of which were repeated. At the same time they rated or ranked each other as to favourability of interpersonal attitudes as well as other attitudes. Over the sixteen-week period the calculation of 'similarity of attitudes' between individuals in terms of statistical indices is statistically significant to a high degree. ('Statistically significant' means that the association between the two rankings/ratings, over the sixteen-week period, has a very low probability indeed of being due to chance factors. It represents in this present case a 'real' degree of similarity.)

Newcomb suggests that not only increased knowledge of

another by observation is likely to lead to a fairly stable index of attraction (between the fifth and fifteenth week, for example, the index varied only fractionally), but that in the interaction process itself certain new qualities concerning the other are elicited by the observer. One does not as a rule reject one's own initiative (which would lead to a lower index of attractiveness), for we attribute to others whom we find rewarding those qualities we value in ourselves.

Though these subjects were of a higher age than that of the normal school age range in Britain, it is likely that many of the same considerations apply, though in the normal day-school

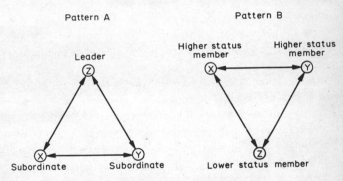

Pattern A   Pattern B

Figure 1.1 Patterns of interaction in triads

milieu the initial formation of these interpersonal perceptions in the dyads will take longer to form, and may not always be as stable and as constant in the absence of the continuous interaction that living together will provide.

2 *The triad.* The next step in size, groups of three (called a *triad*), changes the interaction situation considerably. Each of the original participants in a group of two has now to consider the behaviour of a third member, and the effect is to change or, in technical terms, *modify* the behaviour of others.

The presence of a third party radically alters the interaction pattern of the group because each member of the original dyad has to take account of the third party's feelings, words and actions in the sharing process that characterises group inter-action. This makes for adjustment and upheaval in which roles and power relations are changed. What was originally a 1+1 situation becomes a 1+2 situation where, in the latter three-person case, the 1 is either the leader or the lower-status member. The triangular representation has social aptness in that the apex can either represent dominance (Pattern A, figure 1.1) or, when inverted, lower status (Pattern B, figure 1.1). As we said above, much behaviour of a more complex nature can be explained by reference to the original dyad. In fact the triad is the first size of group which can be described as balanced or imbalanced. A balanced or stable triad can be so characterised when all three members are positively attracted to share one-to-one relations with each other. Where members are not so attracted, the triad is technically termed unstable. Whether stable or unstable our figure still reveals the essential nature of the triad.

3 *Four or more.* Increases in the size of the group, especially once it reaches double figures, lead to much more complex patterns of interaction. Participation becomes more difficult and what is said freely face to face in a two-person or three-person grouping may not be said when others are watching, or may be said badly or inappropriately. The speaker may be apprehensive as to how the group will receive him and his words. Verbal interaction in larger groups, too, becomes confined to a few members, since the proceedings would become interminable if everyone spoke. There is a tendency to present a *public image* on the part of the verbally active group members and to interact in a special way with other group members partly arising from the *dominance* and *higher status* that such members are accorded by them. Outside the large group the interaction between a high-status and low-status member can revert to the ordinary dyadic pattern.

Classroom group behaviour These observations have quite a degree of applicability to children's behaviour in classroom groups. Such groups exhibit in the behaviour of their pupils the characteristics described, though the teacher is inevitably in the most dominant, verbally active role. However, certain pupils have the same tendencies to dominate discussion and exhibit generally forceful behaviour, while others make few attempts at communicating with others and some may even appear inhibited and withdrawn, displaying what are termed *recessive behaviours.* On the other hand many such withdrawn children are restored to apparent 'normality' in the smaller group just as was the case in the hypothetical group we described. This situation gives psychological backing to the importance of small-group teaching and learning methods — not as a passing fad or whim of fashion but as a form of learning unit that is likely to make the task of the learner easier and the teacher's part in the learning process more effective.

Cohesiveness in classroom groups

In describing group processes thus far it appears obvious that some groups have a greater degree of 'closeness' or 'common sense of purpose' than others. This quality is labelled *cohesiveness* and might be summarised as the 'characteristic of the group in which the forces acting on members to remain in the group are greater than the total forces acting on them to leave' (Davis 1969). A highly cohesive group would be one in which members enjoy interacting with each other and receiving mutual support, and one in which members want to make some kind of sacrifice to maintain its existence. Second, the tasks or goals of such a highly cohesive group would be those that for the most part were in tune with the tasks or goals of the individuals comprising it.

Sherif and Sherif's experiment   Though there will be exceptions, success generally increases morale and team spirit and hence cohesiveness. Sherif and Sherif (1953) report their study in which they allowed twenty-four twelve-year-old boys at a summer camp to form informal groups on arrival and as they got to know each other during the first day or two. After several days they were assigned to new groups in which only about a third of their friends from the informal groups (as revealed by questionnaires) were included. At the end of five days, during which each group shared pleasurable work and leisure experiences, a second questionnaire showed a shift in friendship patterns — the new grouping revealing much the same proportion of friendship, in fact being highly cohesive. Cohesiveness can then, theoretically at least, be manipulated by a careful arrangement of success–failure experiences.

Though a success generally acts as a cohesive influence, failure also acts in this way when the failure can be attributed to the threatened presence or intervention of an external party. This threat tends to unite a group — at least for the duration of the threat. This is likely, then, to be a fairly short-term influence and its persistence as a permanent source of cohesion fairly limited.

Positive and negative cohesiveness Cohesiveness can act among classroom groups in either a *positive* or *negative* way. Generally the influence is likely to be a *positive* one, in that if children are generally motivated to the class's work goals then the more cohesive the classroom group the greater the degree of involvement with the work and the more work that will be done. However, if the children are not motivated in any marked degree then cohesiveness will have the opposite effect, that is, the general unity of the children will operate to ensure a lower degree of involvement with the work and the production of less work. If cohesiveness ensures that nothing succeeds like success, then it similarly ensures that nothing fails like failure. Both states can be contagious, and it is the basic attitudes of the children that determine how cohesiveness operates.

COHESIVENESS IN DIFFERENT TYPES OF SCHOOL
Obviously the attitudes of children (and their parents) in a fee-paying independent school, for example, are in general somewhat different from those children in an inner-city area state school with poor housing and general social deprivation. Cohesiveness may of course operate in both. It certainly will in

the fee-paying independent school because parents, teachers and children will share a common purpose as to what they are about — but it may not in either case always be cohesiveness to a positive end.

The type of cohesiveness in the 'deprived' school has been well portrayed in films like *The Blackboard Jungle* about such an institution in New York. There it operated to produce the group mentality of low work standards, plenty of aggression between pupils to teachers and forceful sanctions on any who sought to operate outside the prevailing standards (or norms) set by the tougher pupils. The traditional type of cohesiveness of the fee-paying independent school has been well documented in the hundreds of stories about boarding-school life and its complex etiquette. In such a situation it operates to produce high work standards, low levels of aggression from pupils to teachers but similarly forceful sanctions on any operating outside the prevailing norms (or standards) set by the socially powerful pupils such as the school prefects. In both cases, however, there have been few literary or film portrayals of cohesiveness operating to produce low work standards in fee-paying schools (such as is often the case in lower-stream 'academic' groups of children) or high work standards in deprived city schools (such as groups of linguistically deprived children successfully acquiring reading and speaking skills). Yet such cases are not uncommon and illustrate that cohesiveness can be both a 'depressive' as well as an 'expansive' influence.

The communication pattern and role behaviour

It has already been noted that a group's behaviour is determined by, or is in technical terms a *function* of, the pattern of *communication* that develops between its members and the resultant structure that is formed in consequence of this communication. *Structure* is the term used of the positions occupied by members as a result of interaction and such interaction takes place when one member communicates with another.

ROLES

Each position has, as a rule, one or more roles associated with it and different roles may have different degrees of status (or prestige) accorded to them by the group. A *role* is *a collection of behaviours that are expected of, or usually shown by, the person occupying a particular position*. The person occupying a particular position is termed a *role incumbent*. Any role incumbent may play his role according to some fixed set of rules laid down by himself or others, or he may create his own way of playing the role without reference to any apparent set of rules, when he is said to be playing such a role *idiosyncratically*. In reading the literature one will find a confusing array of the definitions of such concepts as position, role, status etc., depending on what loyalty a particular writer owes to a particular discipline — psychology, sociology, anthropology and so on. Those given here are primarily psychological definitions but will share much common ground with other disciplines, while retaining their own distinct psychological 'flavour'.

Roles and positions in classroom structures If we look at a classroom group in terms of these definitions, we see that its structure consists of the interactions between two basic positions — teacher and pupil. There is usually one teacher interacting with a particular number of pupils over a fixed period of time but in certain circumstances, e.g. in the process of team teaching, two or more teachers may interact with one common set of pupils over the same period. The roles of teacher and pupil are accorded different *statuses* both by tradition and by the age and developmental differences between the two parties. The statuses are traditionally based on independence (the teacher) and dependence (the pupil), though the relation is not necessarily that of superior and inferior (other than in the knowledge, skill etc., based on the age etc., differences) or that of master and servant. The partial demise of the term schoolmaster and schoolmistress perhaps reflects this shift of emphasis. However, its retention in certain places such as fee-paying independent schools and in the name of both male and female teachers' professional associations shows, I would suggest, a different conception of what the status of the position is assumed to be on the part of those groups.

The roles, or the collection of behaviours expected, or the behaviours actually shown, of teacher and pupil will vary enormously depending upon different settings or institutions. However, in general it might be said that *teachers would be expected as a minimum part of their role* to have adequate knowledge of their subject matter, to know something of how children learn and develop and to be able to devise appropriate learning–teaching experiences in the light of those two considerations. Pupils would be expected as a minimum part of their role to be interested in being learners, to develop the skills of listening to a teacher's exposition of a topic and to acquire the skills of reading, writing about and understanding subject matter, as well as developing some skill with numbers.

It is not surprising that these *roles* are not always so interpreted or, more technically, *played*, or indeed are seen to be very different in some cases from those described. These expectations are theoretical descriptions of what the role concepts 'teacher' and 'pupil' entail, and the very minimum description of behaviours appropriate to the learning society as traditionally conceived in our cultural pattern. The discrepancies between these as psychological concepts and what actually happens will vary according to the particular setting. The teaching behaviours of, for example, some headteachers of fee-paying 'progressive' schools will not necessarily embrace in detail or in sequence what has been outlined — though teachers of whatever persuasion will correspond in some degree to the role expectations described. Some 'progressive' heads, for example, might have said that pupils could devise their own learning experiences rather than the teacher doing so. Indeed the very meaning of the word 'progressive' in this context means 'progress towards a pupil's self-determination in both academic and personal affairs'. In the general area of pupil behaviours these role definitions would not embrace either the case of the truanting pupil, for example, who may not be interested in learning or in acquiring particular academic skills; but since truanting pupils are in the minority, descriptions of their role behaviour will not constitute the norm or the generally accepted standard.

Of course such descriptions as those of teacher and pupil may be said to confirm the existing social order and act as conservative forces inhibiting change. Psychology itself is sometimes similarly accused, not without reason (e.g. Ingleby 1974). Nevertheless the descriptions hold good for the majority of the role incumbents so described. Taking the case of truanting, until a large minority of school-age pupils are so acting their roles, such behaviour will always be seen as idiosyncratic, meaning, as was said earlier, playing the role without reference to any set of rules.

INTERACTION PROCESSES

Reference has already been made to the fact of interaction. Any identifiable incident of group behaviour involves interaction. Interaction theory, stemming from developments in the fifties — Bales (1950) and Homans (1950), for example, providing seminal contributions — is only one of a number of systems or orientations used to describe group processes. Cartwright and Zander (1969) list eight distinct systems, though investigators in the field are unlikely to be tied exclusively to only one, often using a number simultaneously. The concepts basic to this interaction approach are *activity, interaction* and *sentiment.* That is to say, the persons engage in overt or seen behaviours (and not in inner thoughts or moods), with others (and not on their own) which are characterised by emotion or feeling. Though such feelings and emotions will be predominantly amicable ones, they will sometimes be of a hostile nature.

Now such interaction processes are the basic stuff of group structure. Given the concepts of position, role, status and the relations or connections between positions, it is easy to see the attraction to theorists of the geometrical or mathematical representation of such relations. The geometrical representation was first given formal shape by Moreno (1953) who developed it as a social-measurement instrument during the First World War in his native Austria, later applying it to therapy and research groups in the United States. Though he came in due course to ascribe to it the status of a new religion, that aspect is less important than its use in the measurement of group behaviour such as Northway and Weld (1967) describe.

Sociometry

Sociometry, in its basic and simplest form, consists of recording the choice of two or more people in a group with whom the

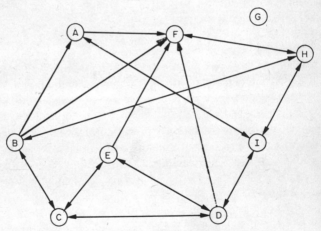

Figure 1.2 Sociogram of a group of junior-school children

subject would most like to be with (or, more technically, *interact with*) in some joint activity such as being in the same work group or the same room. From the collected choices it is possible to plot the structure of the whole group diagrammatically or geometrically. Such diagrams are called *sociograms*. Similarly group members could be asked to write down the names of two or more people with whom they would not want to interact. Hence the diagrammatic structure can show both positive and negative relations.

A typical example of a sociogram appears in figure 1.2. This is an actual sociogram of a group of nine children in a junior school in South London with whom I did some experimental work a few years ago. Each child was asked to write down the names of some other children in the group with whom he would like to work on painting scenery for a school play. The positive choice of one child for another is indicated by an arrow thus→. On looking at the sociogram it will be seen that in some cases there is a mutual choice of partners such as of A by I and of I by A. This is indicated by a double arrow thus←→.

DEFINITION OF RELATIONSHIPS IN A SOCIOGRAM

Within such a relatively complex sociogram, smaller units of relationships reveal themselves and these are termed *stars, mutual pairs, chain structures, cliques* and *isolates*. We shall now explain these terms by reference to the sociogram itself. In the sociogram, F is the most popular child or *star* receiving five out of a possible ten choices. B and C, and C and D, are two examples of *mutual pairs*, that is their choices are reciprocal. (There are other mutual pairs of course within the sociogram as well as these.) *Chain structures*, such as the relation to the star F of B through C, D, I and H are fairly common to most sociograms, as are *cliques* or subgroups, as represented by the relation of C, E and F. G is an *isolate*, that is, he chooses no one and no one chooses him.

It is of course important to realise that we have not dealt with the operation of negative choices which would provide another set of perceptions parallel to the positive ones. The nature of isolation, for example, is much more complex than its simple, positive representation here, embracing both neglect and rejection as well as simply being the result of receiving and making no choices. Then, too, we might represent more clearly the smaller units of the group's relationships, such as *cliques*, by extracting them from the main sociogram. In passing we might note that such units of social interaction have a whole extensive terminology to themselves representing not only the 'liking' structure of the sociogram but also the *communication networks* between persons in a group.

The advantages of such pictures are obviously that they aid our intuition as to what group structures are really like. Nevertheless the construction of such diagrams is often misleading because certain critical factors can be missed in the attempt to achieve a simple structure. Short or long lines between subjects, page arrangement, heavy or light type can easily combine to give a false impression of a group's structure. Then too, as group sizes rise, the maze effect created by the criss-cross of lines and symbols as well as an equitable spatial arrangement makes fair representation practically impossible. This would particularly be the case in a class group of thirty pupils, for example.

MATRICES

An alternative to sociograms is to employ matrices. While sacrificing the intuitive advantages of sociograms, they enable a greater degree of precision to be achieved since the relations can

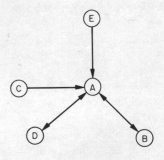

Figure 1.3 Relations between five persons in sociogrammatic form

be more exactly represented. Figure 1.3 indicates the relations between five persons in sociogram form such as has been described already, while figure 1.4 shows a matrix form of the same relationship. It will be seen in the matrix form that the rows of the matrix represent the sender, the columns the receiver. Each box or cell has either a 1, representing the presence of a relation between two persons, or a 0, representing no relation between them. Reciprocal relations can be seen by inspecting the matrix (e.g. A and D have a reciprocal relationship, A and C do not). While the illustration here is a

		Receiver				
		A	B	C	D	E
Initiator	A		1	0	1	0
	B	1		0	0	0
	C	1	0		0	0
	D	1	0	0		0
	E	1	0	0	0	

Figure 1.4 Relations between five persons in matrix form (after Davis 1969)

simple one involving five persons, the advantages of the matrix representation over geometrical representation with large numbers are fairly self-evident. Such matrices can also be used to chart the group in action, namely by representing the strength or frequency of a relation between persons in numerical terms other than 1 or 0. These allow mathematical operations with such numbers to be performed which can sometimes reveal new patterns and trends of group interaction (Harary, Norman and Cartwright 1965; Lindzey and Bryne 1968).

STRENGTHS AND WEAKNESSES OF THE TWO TECHNIQUES

While the matrix representation of group structure will not be of immediate practical use in the classroom, but is rather a research tool, there is little doubt that the sociogram method of representation is of value to the functioning of any classroom group. Provided that pupil members of the group can be assured that their choices will remain confidential to the teacher only, it can be perceived by them as a pleasant way of arranging their environment to their own advantage. It is representative of the child's viewpoint, as opposed to the teacher's, and can give valuable information to enable the teacher to organise learning groups so as to avoid conflict and confusion. For example, a child viewed as unpopular by a teacher for any reason may be seen to be quite popular with his peers, and such information is most useful. The sociogram also reveals subgroups and the relations or lack of relations between each of them. Such groupings are not always evident to a teacher merely by observing his class.

The disadvantages are that the sociogram gives a picture of the classroom group in terms of liking and/or rejecting or 'positive/negative' rather than the 'no firm or particular choice' pattern that characterises much group interaction. Like many types of answer arising from the social situation in which the question is asked, it imposes the obligation on a pupil to make a definite answer. If he does not, he may well feel with no justification 'isolated' and 'antisocial'. In asking for particular choices the tendency on the part of the group is to make them, whether or not they correspond to a subject's 'true' feelings. Another disadvantage to which reference has already been made is the difficulty of representing relations between large numbers of subjects. Then, too, many teachers, perhaps rightly, have objections on moral grounds to the negative form of the question, namely asking children to say with whom they would not want to work or sit or interact generally.

CORRESPONDENCE TO REALITY

In this discussion the question of how far a person's choices in a sociometric test correspond to his actual desire for association have only been lightly touched on. Certainly the subjects of his choice will usually be acceptable to him, but the correspondence between his expressed choice, and the 'success' of that choice in harmonious relations, is not always or necessarily a perfect correspondence. As Newcomb's experiment that we have already discussed showed, when 'free' choices in a group were forcibly changed by outsiders and monitored over a period, the 'forced' choices of individuals were eventually as 'liked' as the 'free' choices had been. It does seem, therefore, that interaction can be both freely and forcibly entered into, and sociograms will represent such interaction favourably on each occasion.

Essentially, then, sociograms are an effective method of illustrating group structures, but only at some levels. They leave a good deal unsaid and what is unsaid can be very important. They are valuable tools in the preliminary identification of the pattern of group interaction but need supplementation by other methods as time passes.

Group norms

Groups develop norms of behaviour which can be regarded as a kind of culture in miniature. Such norms will govern the styles of social behaviour which are approved and admired. Anyone who fails to conform is placed under pressure to do so, and if he does not he is rejected. (Argyle 1972)

In a general sense a *norm* is *a standard against which the appropriateness or otherwise of a behaviour or set of behaviours is judged.* These norms may be *general*, that is applying to life at large, or *particular*, that is applying only to members of a particular group. Norms are synonymous with regularities, and human life would indeed be chaotic if regularities were absent. The regularities, or norms, of group life that chiefly concern us here are those that are recognised by the participants in interaction sequences, by those in fact who are in some way affected by those norms.

FORMAL AND INFORMAL NORMS

Many of such norms, whether applied to society or groups, are *formal* (and sometimes even legal) ones, and many are *informal* ones. Some are specific, some are general. There is often a moral dimension to them such as 'ought', 'should', even 'right and wrong', and yet sometimes they are never actually stated in words. As Kelvin (1969) says, 'In essence a group consists of people who know, or believe they know, what to expect from one another'. In general, however, norms define the situation in which the regularity applies, and they contain descriptions of what the participants are to think, feel and do in the particular situation they define and to which participants these descriptions apply. For example, it might be a generally agreed norm that pupils in a school class do not break up the furniture or assault the teacher, and similarly that the teacher does not assault the pupils. These rules or regularities, however, are not always written down but obviously exert strong influences on the way teachers and pupils behave. It is interesting to note too that norms often have overtones of prohibition — 'Do not do this', 'Do not do that'. Norms are seldom (perhaps too seldom) seen publicly, or perceived privately, as positive and encouraging in tone.

Attitudes   The regularities that norms embody become the objects of *attitudes,* that is *members approve or disapprove of them with varying degrees of feeling or intensity.* Following Thibaut and Kelly (1959) it can be said that a group norm exists to the extent that the group members share positive attitudes to any such regularity. That is, they share such attitudes in the sense that they agree, and are aware that they agree, that the regularity has the force of law in the group and in its application to group members. Group norms differ from other shared attitudes in that they represent shared acceptance of rules, which rules in turn become influential in determining how group members perceive, think, feel and act.

PSYCHOLOGICAL CONSEQUENCES OF NORMS

Newcomb, Turner and Converse (1965) note the psychological consequences of regularities or norms:

The psychological counterpart of an observed regularity is

the expectation, with some degree of certainty, that an event will occur: the sun will rise tomorrow morning, for example, or the driver of a car will stop when the traffic light is red. When, as in the latter case, we are dealing with a regularity that is also a rule concerning human behaviour, its psychological counterpart includes not just the expectation that the rule will probably be observed but also the anticipation of consequences of observing it, or of violating it. Such consequences are sometimes automatic, in the sense that other people's intervention is not needed to make them occur; if, for example, one does not accept the rule that the bus leaves the terminal precisely at noon, one suffers the consequence of missing it. Or, to give a different kind of illustration, all human societies have rules concerning the use of words; the consequence of not accepting such rules is that one will have difficulty in understanding others and in making oneself understood.

What the preceding authors emphasise is that any rule, whether explicit or implicit, depends on *sanctions* for its implementation. These sanctions may be either positive, in the form of some kind of reward, or negative, in the form of some kind of punishment. Group norms, in fact, flow from the acceptance of such rules as legitimate and proper sanctions on individual members. Such rules persist if they are seen as supporting relationships that are desired by the members. If the group's morale is high, sanctions are more likely to be positive and the rules will virtually enforce themselves. Only if morale falls will sanctions tend to be negative and in turn evoke stricter and more detailed rules.

CLASSROOM NORMS
In terms of the classroom group the question of norms figures widely but such considerations are often, as we have stressed above, 'dressed up' in the guise of sanctions being regarded as actions, punitive actions usually, against pupils. This seems to me to be looking at norm formation the wrong way round. The

norms are, as we said, sustained by sanctions which, in groups with high morale and/or with groups carrying out their tasks effectively, are virtually self-enforcing.

So, for example, in a group of infant children with a high level of pre-reading skill the behaviours an observer might record would most likely be those of praise, encouragement and approval of the children by the teacher. From the children it is likely that both their oral and written activities would figure prominently as shown by their ready enthusiasm in answering questions and in the large amount of written and activity material covered. *In theory* the norms of behaviour consist of positive interaction in an appropriate learning context. *In practice* the norms are the same, that is they represent what actually happens. The correspondence between theory and practice is close and the group acts together and is in fact cohesive. The sanctions are positive, virtually unnoticed and in fact self-enforcing.

On the other hand in a group of low-ability sixteen-year-olds (by definition almost certainly keen to leave school) the behaviours an observer might record could well consist principally, as far as the teacher was concerned, in his displeasure with pupils, as shown, for example, by his severe tone of voice and his detaining pupils at break-times. From the pupils it is likely that both their uncooperative attitudes and their apparent lack of interest in learning would result in hostility to the teacher and to each other. *In theory* the norms of behaviour are broadly the same as with younger children, namely positive interaction in appropriate learning situations. *In practice*, however, much of the interaction would be negative and the appropriateness of the learning situation at times questionable. The theoretical norms of the group would not correspond to what actually happens. The correspondence between theory and practice is remote and the group does not act together, for it is not cohesive. The sanctions are basically all negative as shown by the criticisms of pupils by the teacher and the hostility of individual pupils to each other, leading to a higher level of aggression throughout the class. If such patterns of behaviour persist over long periods of time the whole scene can become one of negation and despair on the part of both teacher and pupil.

This situation is a good example of the contradiction between what is thought to happen, and what actually does happen in educational institutions. This theme of contradiction between *public* and *private* behaviour is one that will recur throughout this book. The strength of norms, as opposed to the sanctions which are needed to make them real, is that their vagueness does allow for both positive as well as negative developments. So school classes of sixteen-year-olds are not inevitably doomed to spend their time in the way described, and many of us know of cases where the norms (positive) accord with the sanctions (positive) at this age level.

SANCTIONS

The concern with sanctions, then, is often perceived by popular commentators on education in the media, for example, not in terms of reinforcing the class group's purpose (the effective learning of the group members), but in a wholly negative way — 'Bash them and they'll learn'. The same attitude characterises much popular comment on both corporal and capital punishment in Britain, where the *retribution element*, 'Bash them', is seen as dominant and not the *element of control*, namely whether in fact such sanctions effectively reduce the rate of crime as compared with other less drastic punishments, such as physical detention and/or personal deprivation, such as not taking part in games.

Value judgements Certainly retribution is probably a justifiable and understandable element in any system of sanctions, within education or outside it, though it will not be for psychologists to determine its correct place. Such determination belongs to the realm of value judgements. *Value judgements* may be defined as *the values judged relevant by society as a whole, or by groups in society, in regard to a social, political or moral issue.* They are judgements upon which social scientists may wish to comment and which they may be called upon to analyse as far as the particular content of these judgements are concerned. However, in their role as social scientists they will not be professionally concerned with determining which value judgements are 'right' and which are 'wrong'; they could of course be concerned in their role as educators with such issues.

Sherif's and Asch's experiments

Of all the aspects of group functioning it is *norm formation* that has developed as a major theoretical interest, and it is not difficult to see why, since norms are the major determinant of how the group functions or fails to function. One of the classic experiments in this regard and one which figures prominently in the literature is that of Sherif (1936). Though performed forty years ago it demonstrated, with a directness that has not been bettered as yet, how group interaction affects individual perception.

SHERIF'S EXPERIMENT

Subjects were placed in a darkened room and asked to observe a stationary pinpoint of light. Under proper laboratory conditions such a light is always perceived to move and this effect (known as the *autokinetic phenomenon*) does not depend on any intervention by the person in charge of the experiment. The subjects were required to estimate the amount of apparent movement of the light, at first individually, and then in groups of two or three. It is important to note the splendid experimental design, for the stimulus is a thoroughly ambiguous one, there being in fact no right answer, and hence the subject has to supply estimates of the light's movement completely from his own perceptions.

In the first part of the experiment the subjects working on their own estimated the light's movement 100 times (called technically 'trials') and they tended to settle their estimates in a very narrow range, though the actual level for each individual varied from around 2 inches or slightly more, to 8 inches or slightly more. A further 100 trials revealed the same results. A person's development of these individual regularities Sherif

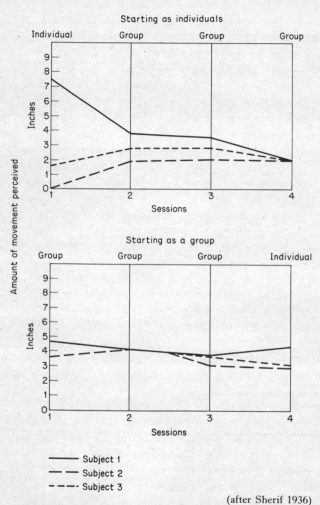

(after Sherif 1936)

Figure 1.5 Effect of group participation on individuals' judgements

called *individual norms.*

In the second part of the experiment the subjects, this time working in groups of two or three, again estimated the light's movement for 100 trials. But on this occasion each subject after each trial announced aloud his judgement of the distance to the other group members. Members of half of the groups had no previous experience of the autokinetic phenomenon, whereas the other half had already built up their individual norms as previously outlined. Both types of members gradually developed *group norms,* that is, as the trials progressed, they came to make judgements closer to those of each other group member. Though norms differed a great deal from group to group, members within each group developed similar individual norms to the others. The pattern is shown in figure 1.5 taken from Sherif's original experiment. (It is also interesting to note, as the second graph indicates, that when members who started out in a group 'went solo' their estimates began to diverge again.)

The convergence towards a common regularity or norm took place without any related conversation or formal decision by the group as to how members should judge the movement. We can perhaps infer with confidence that each subject knew that his colleague, or colleagues (in the three man group), accepted more or less the same standard of judgement. Each member was not just solely influenced by the other; each was influenced by something jointly created through interaction — a *norm,* in fact.

Educational implications   If we look at Sherif's study in an educational context we can see that it has a number of implications. These arise because to pupils, and sometimes to teachers, parts of the curriculum and certainly the morality aspect of pupils' learning (what is 'right' and 'wrong') are, in the current state of society, very ambiguous indeed. Pupils faced with an ambiguous situation (created perhaps either by the teacher or by other groups of pupils) are inclined to depend on one another for what they should do. The group consensus that evolves as to the 'appropriate' action in the particular situation will often carry over into other behaviours either within or outside the group. Both pupils and teachers may be unaware of the processes involved but the power of such consensual agreement to influence behaviour can be seen to be very real. The further issue that arises is this. Given the ambiguous situation, where pupils will be likely to choose a common consensual solution, what happens when the problem or stimulus is not ambiguous but is definite? Many teacher initiatives are definite, whatever else they may or may not be — 'Do this', 'Do that' and so on.

The problem of the non-ambiguous stimulus had suggested itself to the social psychologists of the late thirties and forties following Sherif's original experiment. How would subjects judge stimuli or problems that had not ambiguity but objective reality about them? Would individuals respond, as in the Sherif experiment, to the norms or regularities of others, or would they rely on the evidence of their own eyes?

ASCH'S EXPERIMENT

Asch (1956) did such a series of experiments in which subjects were asked to judge which one of three straight lines was the same length as a 'standard' line. On their own, subjects rarely made a mistake, but when in the company of others who had been previously told before the experiment to call out the wrong answer, only about a quarter of the subjects remained uninfluenced and called out the correct answer. A half yielded to the group's (wrong) answer an average of three times out of twelve trials, a quarter yielded an average of nine times out of the twelve.

In the original experiment the subjects were confronted with a unanimous majority of eight calling out the wrong answer but Asch found that reducing the majority to three against the subject was quite as effective in producing conformity to the wrong answer. When the subject was joined by one other member of the group who gave the correct answer, however, the subject also stuck to it despite the majority's adherence to the wrong answer. If, however, the other member half-way through the twelve trials suddenly began (as in some cases he was instructed to do) giving the majority's wrong answer, then the subject too succumbed and his error rate increased substantially. It was clear that the presence of a partner did strengthen a person's resolve to resist the majority but it did not completely eliminate the pressures arising from the action of that majority.

Educational implications   Perhaps the educational implications of the Asch experiment are not as immediately obvious as in the Sherif case. The conflict that the Asch experiment revealed was that between objective fact and group pressure. The group pressure of the majority was seen to triumph over individual judgement. Subjects did not, on the whole, perceive the deception. Interviews conducted with them afterwards showed that while they were aware that their perceptions of the length of the line were different they concluded the majority were probably right — 'It usually is'. Some were not aware that their perceptions were different — they merely heard what the majority reported without 'taking it in'. (True of much teacher talk in classrooms!) A minority were aware that their perceptions were different, felt the majority to be wrong, but decided to go along with the group so as not to appear out of step.

The latter behaviour is often typical of pupils' behaviour in subjects like mathematics and science. In such subjects pupils often accept uncritically some answer, perhaps explained by a teacher or fellow pupil (which explanation may be wrong, even if the final answer is correct). They do not ask for more guidance because to do so would be to present themselves to the explainer as out of step, awkward, or, not very bright. The implications of the Asch experiment appear to me to be the tolerance of, and the attempt to understand, the minority opinions of pupils. Though at times as erroneous as the views and perceptions of some of Asch's subjects, these opinions are often thought to be right by the pupils and hence need an understanding ear, followed by the teacher's explanation as to why they are wrong. Likewise a pupil's assent to the explanation of a particular idea is not to be taken as implying he necessarily understands that idea.

2

Person perception and classroom communication

Introduction

The process whereby impressions of other people are formed is called *person perception*. All group interaction is rooted in this process. It is important to emphasise that, although the term *person perception* has come into common use, the term is really something of a misnomer because *perception*, as used in physiological psychology, implies the use of direct information from the senses. That is to say we decide on the basis of information we record by the eye, for example, that two objects are the same size, or on information recorded by the ear that two sounds are dissimilar. With the perception of people our recording apparatus is not used in the same way. We may see and hear others but our impression of them is much more complex than the process of distinguishing the size of objects or the pitch of sounds. For example, in assessing persons we may proceed on the basis of statements by others or of vague knowledge about the person or even from our reaction to any personal peculiarities that the person may possess. We might have some fixed idea in our minds such as 'red-haired people are hot tempered' and fit our perception to our preconceived ideas, so that when we see a red-haired person we perceive him as 'hot tempered' without any evidence to confirm that perception. Certainly in all cases we are likely to have some 'fitting' to do, since no perception of another occurs in a vacuum but is carried out with our existing perceptual equipment at both the *sensory* level ('her eyes are green') and at the *affective* level ('I trust all

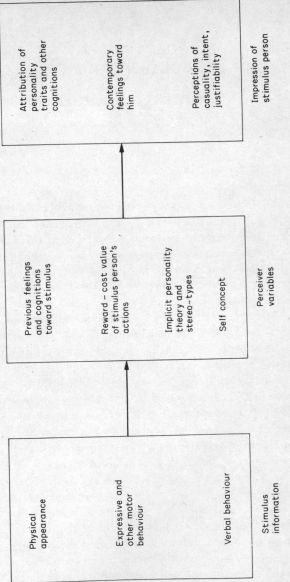

Physical appearance

Expressive and other motor behaviour

Verbal behaviour

Stimulus information

Previous feelings and cognitions toward stimulus

Reward - cost value of stimulus person's actions

Implicit personality theory and stereo-types

Self concept

Perceiver variables

Attribution of personality traits and other cognitions

Contemporary feelings toward him

Perceptions of casuality, intent, justifiability

Impression of stimulus person

(after Secord and Backman 1964)

Figure 2.1 Factors in forming impressions of a person's personality

green-eyed girls, hence I trust her'). So while we shall continue to use the term 'person perception as a convenient one, it is important to emphasise that such acts of perception are rather different from what classic experimental psychology would mean by the term. The nature of the process of person perception is illustrated in figure 2.1.

Forming impressions of people

Stimulus information   The left-hand block of figure 2.1 outlines the stimulus information that begins the process. In this discussion and subsequent discussions we shall call the person doing the observing *the observer*, and the person being observed *the person*. We shall describe the process in terms of the figure statically as though the person is being observed by the observer without the person reacting. In real life, however, the observer's observation would produce a reaction in the person which, while not altering the dimensions we are describing, would make their 'summing up' much more difficult. Obviously the physical appearance of the person is a clear initial stimulus and can exert an overwhelming influence on the observer — blotting out all other impressions. Then too the expressive movement of the person conveys another set of clues as to the person's nature. How he stands and uses his hands and how he walks are all part of this stimulus area. Finally what the person says and how he says it provide yet another stimulus. It is important to emphasise again that, while these three areas are broken down here and described one by one, they occur almost instantly in the observer. He is not likely to assess them in sequence in his mind — 'his personality is . . . his verbal behaviour is . . .' — for much of the analysis will be instantaneous and immediate.

Perceiver variables   The middle block of figure 2.1 shows the critical areas that *the observer* entertains concerning *the person*. The observer's previous feelings towards, and his present knowledge of, the person operate here, that is to say the observer incorporates in his view anything he may have heard or seen of the person.

The second, 'reward–cost value', is particularly important since if most relations are held to be *transactional* ones (where exchange of personalities occur) the reward–cost aspect is paramount. By reward–cost is meant the balance between the observer's association or interaction with the person bringing pleasure (reward) at the price of time, effort, consideration etc. (cost). All interactional relations are really determined by the balance of reward–cost, though the balance between them, at least in the long term, is not necessarily equal. Some individuals in relations with another appear to make huge efforts (costs) for apparently little pleasure (reward), other individuals apparently make little effort yet appear to receive much pleasure.

The third element is bound up with implicit personality theories and with 'stereotypes' to which reference will later be made. Finally the observer's conception of himself is important, since he is unlikely to pursue any relationship that does not enhance his own *self-concept*. (A person's *self-concept* might briefly be defined as the feelings and expectations a person has about himself.) If, for example, the observer is a member of a club he is unlikely to associate with the person for any length of time if the person thinks clubs and club life in general to be a lot of archaic rubbish. Unless the observer can convert the person to his point of view the relationship would be too painful to the observer's self-concept as a clubman. Of course, if the other rewards of association were so strong, the observer might change his self-concept and cease to be a clubman or, conversely, convert the person to club life himself.

Impression of stimulus person　　The right-hand block of figure 2.1 illustrates various aspects of the impression formed by *the observer*. He attributes to *the person* various personality traits and other 'known' factors, for example the person may be seen as introverted or extroverted, temperamentally warm or cold, rich or poor and so on. The observer has feelings of like or dislike, respect etc. towards the person and forms impressions as to whether these feelings are caused by situational factors or whether they arise from intentional behaviour on the person's part.

Teachers' and pupils' impressions of each other

The whole range of the factors employed in forming impressions of personality are very much in evidence both on the part of a teacher when he first meets his pupils and on the part of the pupils when they first meet their teacher. The process, of course, continues for a longer time than in a one-to-one relationship since it is often a one-to-thirty or more relationship. Referring again to figure 2.1, physical appearance and verbal behaviour are particularly important since they obviously influence interaction. Perception of them is immediate and sets the tone of much that is to follow. In terms of the 'reward–cost value' the teacher, within his professional relationship with pupils, has much the same calculation to make as in any other relationship. Teaching–learning is a *transaction* and, while the demands of the teacher's role are traditionally unlimited in theory, in practice the teacher has to balance rewards (pupils' progress) with costs (spreading myself and my time among forty pupils).

The *teacher's self-concept*, too, will of course determine in some part how he sees himself in terms of cost and rewards. When we were earlier discussing the clubman's self-concept we noted that he was likely to associate only with people who supported or enhanced it and certainly not with any who actively rejected it. A teacher often has to associate, and is charged with assisting in the learning of people, namely his pupils, who may actively reject his previously formed self-concept. Pupils have similarly to associate with teachers though their part of the transaction, willingness to learn, is not tied to monetary rewards or any paid responsibility. Though a teacher seldom rejects a pupil's self-concept (unless the pupil persists in antisocial behaviour), problems with pupils can arise precisely because they may feel their teacher is not really in sympathy with their developing self-concepts. This is generally characteristic of older rather than of younger pupils, but the resultant conflict between pupil and teacher emphasises the peculiar difficulties and, if resolved, the peculiar satisfactions of the job.

The impressions of the pupils (the perceivers) will be very mixed at first and, unlike the case of one-to-one relationships, a group norm soon emerges from a class of pupils as to what teachers in general should be, whether this teacher in fact fits that norm. (What above we describe dispassionately as 'feelings ensuing from situational or intentional behaviours'.) The impression-forming process in a one-to-thirty relationship (one teacher to thirty children) is thus seen on the part of the perceivers (the thirty children) to be of a different kind from that involved in one-to-one relations.

SOCIAL TECHNIQUES

Argyle (1972) uses the term *social techniques* for all the things we do, both verbally and non-verbally, deliberately or unconsciously, to influence others in the course of social intercourse. He describes seven different kinds of social act, namely *bodily contact* (such as shaking hands), *physical proximity and position, gestures, facial expressions, eye movements, non-linguistic aspects of speech* and *speech* itself as the basic elements which are integrated into larger units of social behaviour in many different ways to form the basis of the techniques we all use in our interpersonal behaviour.

So immediately two people meet they bring their respective social techniques into action. Each person of course will have several sets of social techniques but will use them and vary them differently. While there may be a basic pattern for each person, which could be called characteristic of that person, the variations upon the basic pattern are many. Young children will have a basic pattern of fairly unco-ordinated acts indulging in all the seven types described (facial expression, bodily contact etc.), often in a random fashion. As they grow older patterns become more stable, for the acquisition and enhancement of social techniques is one of the signs of the transition first from childhood to adolescence, and second from adolescence to adulthood. Of course such acquisition and enhancement is likely to go on for a person's whole life, and certainly prolonged social contact in either a professional or private role will call for such development as a condition of its continuation. Where such development is absent, relationships may cease or run down.

When two people meet for the first time the process described earlier in the chapter begins. First impressions are fairly important, for each person categorises the other initially on what each perceives as an individual to be important and, if interaction proceeds and is not broken off, on what both then perceive jointly to be important. These categories are both alike and dissimilar and range over many areas — job or profession, age, general social background, particular interests and so on. Depending on what each wants from the relationship, each will employ the appropriate social techniques necessary to achieve the end he has in view. For example, if one of them is seeking a job from the other he will try to present himself as eager, as suitable — probing from the prospective employer conditions about the job before deciding perhaps whether he should either (1) press on and place himself before the prospective employer as a real applicant, (2) seek more information about the job before 'pressing' his candidature, (3) decide he doesn't want the job anyway but go along with the interaction for a while before formally withdrawing or (4) withdraw abruptly or even rudely. This type of pattern is fairly common in a lot of meetings between individuals, especially if some particular end is at stake whether that end is immediate, as for example a job, or long term, as perhaps a possible or eventual engagement or marriage. Meetings of any kind between persons can be termed *interactions, interaction sequences* or *encounters.*

If we examine, in terms of Argyle's seven areas, the progression of such a relationship as it might occur, it will be possible to see how the basic elements of social behaviour are employed to initiate particular social techniques. Apart from a formal introduction there is likely to be little *bodily contact* apart from the initial shaking of hands — at least between members of the same sex. *Physical proximity* and position will vary according to the conditions; for example, in an introduction at a cocktail party proximity is likely to be closer than at a formal interview for a job. *Gestures* (which term embraces all bodily movement and not only the movement of the hands) vary very widely from culture to culture. There is far more body movement than the participants themselves might suppose. Head nodding, nose scratching and hand movements, for instance, all occur continuously, some connected with the interaction that is proceeding, as with head nodding, others being involuntary and apparently unrelated to it. *Facial expressions* may give some clues as to the emotional state of the participants but can be part of their normal expression. A half-shut eye and a lowered mouth are not necessarily an indication that the interaction is becoming difficult.

Eye movements or *gaze* are both very important in sustaining interaction, and the exchange of glances by the participants dictates the tone and ensures the continuance of the interaction. The prime reason for people looking at each other is to collect information rather than to send it, though, as Argyle (1975) has recently pointed out, a gaze can be decoded in a number of ways. In looking at a person I may seek only to know if he is awake. He, on the other hand, may perceive my gaze as conveying a threat, conveying liking or conveying dominance. Gaze is closely linked with speech and is an important accompaniment to the next social act, non-linguistic aspects of speech.

Non-linguistic aspects of speech is the term applied to the patterns of speech between people — how often one interrupts another, how fast they speak when conversing, their rate of speech errors and so on. If one looks at speech in terms of an exchange theory, then apart from any linguistic implications the ebb and flow of speech patterns is a good index of, say, how dominant one partner is over the other, how much one yields to the other and how hesitant one partner is in the interaction process.

Finally, of course, *speech* itself is the highest form of communication and the most complex of the means of interaction. Animal noises communicate only emotional states and status, whereas speech is learnt, can recall past events or anticipate future ones and has a form and a grammatical structure. While the first five areas are common to man and animals, it is the added dimension of speech which gives these behavioural acts a special meaning. The differences between individuals or groups of individuals are often seen primarily in terms of their facility in speech. Since this skill is developed by formal education, speech patterns and the skills themselves are often outward and visible signs of the milieu from which a person comes, and one of the major dimensions people latch on to in the encounters such as were described earlier. Bernstein (1961 and 1971), for example, has compared the structure of speech in different environments and indicated how differences in usage are associated with membership of different social classes.

Bernstein's concern has been to compare the structure and the use of language among 'working-class' persons and 'middle-class' persons. The former use what he first termed *public language* (later replaced by *restricted code*), the latter *formal language* (later replaced by *elaborated code*). *Public language* is rigid in syntax, and its formal possibilities for verbal organisation are restricted. *Formal language* is fluid in syntax possibilities, and its formal possibilities for sentence organisation are wide, leading to classification and explication on a much wider scale than with public language. The theories, fascinating as they are, are too detailed to recapitulate at length here, but the substance of Bernstein's lament — namely that restricted codes blunt the natural curiosity of the child — has far-reaching consequences for teachers. Teachers are generally, by upbringing or by desire, users of the elaborated code, and many teachers' work lies with working-class children who have only the restricted code. It is another important area of differentiation between teachers and children that can at times result in a conflict that neither party desires.

Argyle (1972) distinguishes three direct uses of speech: (1) to ask questions, (2) to convey information and (3) to influence the behaviour of others. These uses are combined in different ways and we shall look later at the various usages of speech forms in connection with particular aspects of the teaching process. Certainly speech is perhaps the most powerful element in interaction generally, determining much of the action and the sequence of action that takes place. However, in teaching, if teachers' verbal and non-verbal signals conflict, pupils are likely to react more to the non-verbal signals since such signals are technically termed more *visible*. We shall return to the matter of *visibility* again later.

SOCIAL ACTS IN TEACHING

In the teaching situation the seven social acts (or six if we leave aside speech for the moment) are obviously the essential personal tools of communication. Let us examine each area a little more closely:

Bodily contact   Bodily contact is likely to be rare; indeed apart from the handshake of senior school leavers or of pupils at prize-givings such contact is fraught with professional danger in our society. Blows inflicted in anger (very understandable too if one has prolonged contact with some children) where corporal punishment is not legally sanctioned, and sometimes even where it is, can lead to charges of criminal assault. Other contacts, such as a teacher putting his arms round a pupil, also run a risk of being technically termed an indecent assault. Hence bodily contact — and this reflects the norms of society at large — is not part of normal social relations.

Physical proximity and position   Physical proximity and position will vary, and certainly some of the informal teaching methods of recent years have been attempts to give greater opportunities for learning in such terms. For example, pupils arranged in small circular groups (as opposed to patterns like four rows of six tables in a rectangle) and the teacher circulating among them, sitting with one group and then with another, represents such an informal pattern, as opposed to the formal pattern of the big raised teacher's desk and chair at the front of the class.

It is important to remember, as Argyle (1975) notes, that 'spatial behaviour is part of social skill'. He continues:

In addition to adopting an appropriate spatial position in relation to another person, social skills may involve arranging the space for a group of people. For example, a school teacher can arrange the desks in a classroom in a number of different ways, producing quite different patterns of interaction.

1 Traditional rows of desks, for teacher-centred sessions with little discussion, or for taking exams.

2 Groups of four desks facing each other, or a library table.

3 A number of pupils in a row behind the teacher's desk, the others facing in a semi-circle, for reading a play.

4 A hollow square, for committee work.

5 Rows of desks, facing on two sides of the room, teacher, in middle with slides, tape-recorder etc., e.g. for a language lesson.

6 A semi-circle of desks, for discussion (Richardson 1967).

Gestures and facial expressions   Gestures and facial expressions are important in teaching, not least because they are often important determinants for a teacher of his class's attitudes and behaviour towards him. Student teachers who have watched videotape recordings of themselves teaching have often been horrified to find they used gestures and facial expressions of whose existence they were unaware — 'No wonder the pupils laughed at me' — and which they could change.

In teaching interaction is complicated by the relatively high number of perceivers of any individual teacher. In a person-to-person exchange gestures and facial expressions are not always noticed consciously. In teaching, however, because of the social distance between teacher and pupil, and because there may be thirty perceivers and not one, any idiosyncrasies can become magnified. These can become the subject of discussion between pupils and can exert an influence on pupils' classroom behaviour — 'Here comes the nose scratcher' — out of all magnitude to the cause. Of course it is important to remember that gestures and facial expressions can operate in a positive way as well, so that teachers are more easily accepted with one set than with another. The training process seems likely to have only a limited effect here, since, while experiences of videotaping may enable a teacher to eliminate 'bad' elements (and this is a step forward), it will not necessarily cultivate good ones. I suspect many elements of this nature are genetically and environmentally too interwoven with our past history for us to be able to change them radically.

Eye movements or gaze   Eye movements or gaze are critical, of course, in teaching because they determine in great part the nature of any kind of interaction. When the teacher talks to the whole class his gaze travels across the pupils continuously, scanning them like a security TV camera in a departmental store and only coming to rest and meeting the particular gaze of a pupil when he either wants a reply from him or speaks to him directly. Unlike the TV camera, however, the teacher's gaze is more rapid in its travel and also in its analysis of pupils' behaviour. While the TV camera has to be stopped while an observer looks more closely at what the shopper is doing, the teacher can make decisions in a split second.

So many decisions concerning pupils' behaviour that have to be made in the stress of the moment are too quick and instinctive to permit a detailed analysis by the teacher. He has to keep control and ensure that naughty or inattentive pupils know they are being noticed. Then too his peripheral vision, that is, the vision 'out of the corner of the eye', will often interfere with his perceptions of a particular incident. Hence he deals with one pupil quickly and perhaps 'wrongly', so as to pass on and quell trouble in another part of the classroom. Of course if he is engaged in a lesson with popular subject matter or content, such as telling a story where all pupils, whatever their intellectual level, can participate, he will find all eyes upon him and pupils will be really interacting continuously.

The advantage of splitting a whole class into smaller teaching groups, apart from any other benefit to the pupils such as permitting them to discuss their work with colleagues, is that the teacher can distribute his gaze more frequently and with greater emphasis and so make pupils feel they are being noticed. The desire for notice, or what is called 'attention seeking', is the cause of much general classroom indiscipline. Often a teacher's gaze is enough to quell incipient trouble, and any system that allows for more of it, such as small-group work, is to be valued when the circumstances are appropriate.

Non-linguistic aspects of speech   Finally, non-linguistic aspects of speech in teaching are particularly good indications as to the type of exchange that is taking place. Research shows that teachers tend to talk in an expository manner too frequently and for too long a period at a time. Many researches show a teacher primarily acting as a talker and talking *at* pupils rather than *with* them. Their value lies in illuminating the teacher's behaviour so that he knows what is happening.

Psychological processes of the perceiver

Given that the main strands of the basic theory of person perception have been outlined, it might now be helpful if we looked at the psychological processes of the perceiver. As Newcomb, Turner and Converse (1965) state, 'whenever you really notice a person (as contrasted with the relative inattention that you give to a casual passer by) you are confronted with a problem.' Probably most of us have not seen our social relationships in these terms but there is little doubt that, if one goes beyond the mere observation of physical characteristics, problems arise, because human behaviour is much more complex and diverse than, for example, among other animal species. You can account for animal behaviour in terms of a few observations and descriptions that will hold good for the majority of situations but human behaviour is variable and inconstant. A person who is perceived to be 'rude' when first seen by you (the perceiver), and labelled thus, may act politely when next seen. If you come to know the person well you could learn that he had bad toothache when you first observed him, which gave rise to his rudeness. Of course humans can veer between extremes of behaviour without experiencing bodily pain but the attribution of descriptive labels can only proceed on what is externally observed at the time, as in this case of 'rudeness' we have described here.

We spoke earlier of the stimuli or cues that caused the person doing the observing (*the observer*) to draw inferences about the behavioural pattern(s) of the person being observed (*the person*). In general first impressions are critical and last indefinitely unless contradicted by later experience. The quality of vividness — as conveyed by those impressions that immediately engage the observer such as bright clothes, a loud voice, a short haircut — is important. The latter example perhaps illustrates the contextual or situational nature of such cues. These days a man's hair worn very short excites comment because the fashion is towards long hair. Twenty years ago it would have been the long hairstyle that was conspicuous. Then, too, a loud voice in church is rather different from a loud voice in a fish market: in the first location it is alien, in the other the norm. The more often an aspect of behaviour is presented, the more we notice it. So if *the person*, for example, frequently presents the stimulus of scratching his own head to *the observer*, such behaviour will gain recognition by the observer. Frequency of presentation gains recognition, and so the observer might attribute to the person the label of 'head scratcher' on the basis of his observation.

Having looked at the stimuli or cues 'given off' by the person, it is useful to consider the perceptual process operating within the observer which determine how he views the person. It is perhaps most important to stress here again that this whole process of person perception is a two-way one. We describe for *illustrative purposes only* how the observer perceives the person as though the observer is 'out there' stationary — acting and behaving as a non-engaged observer. This could be misleading. While the observer is engaged in perceiving the person, the person is doing the same with the observer, and these simultaneous acts of perception can cause problems in assessing the accuracy of the perception of either party. As soon as the person perceives that the observer is perceiving him, he is likely to make changes in his behaviour peculiar to the particular situation, changes which he would not make if another third person were perceiving him. Perception does not take place in a vacuum. However, experimental studies can give the impression that it does. For example, two well-tried experimental techniques consist of (1) showing pictures of people to subjects and (2) giving descriptions of physical types to subjects, and in each case asking each subject to write down his perceptions of the pictures or descriptions for eventual analysis. Both such techniques can tend to give the impression that accurate perception does take place in a vacuum. We shall return to the question of accuracy again later.

SENSORY DEPRIVATION — AND ASSOCIATIVE PROCESSES

Obviously in looking at how *the observer* sees *the person* the condition of the observer will vary according to different circumstances. The observer may be hungry or tired or annoyed, in which case he will view the person differently from when he (the observer) is rested, replete and at peace with himself. The way in which the senses directly influence person perception can be seen dramatically in the fairly extreme phenomenon of *sensory deprivation* which has figured prominently in the contemporary political scene. This is the well-known technique of depriving a prisoner of the use of sensory stimulation so as to mould him to the designs of his captors. The identity of the prisoner is assaulted.

Feshback and Singer (1957) reported their experiment on sixty students who were shown together a film of a man working. Forty students, who formed the experimental group, received a number of electric shocks under the impression that the shocks were stimuli aimed at distracting them from giving attention to the film while they watched it. Twenty, who formed a control group, did not. (A control group means a group matched with one other, or with several others, in an experiment who do not experience the experimental condition, in this case electric shocks.) After viewing the film both groups were questioned about the likely personality of the man in the film. Those who had received shocks (the experimental group) attributed neurotic characteristics to the man in the imaginary situations posed in the questions at a much higher statistically significant level than did the control group. So the subjects who received shocks attributed the same emotional states to the person being judged. This 'carry over' played a prominent part in the experimental group's person perception. Conversely, the 'carry over' of pleasant experiences will similarly induce tranquil and pleasurable symptoms rather than the painful ones quoted in the experiment.

STEREOTYPES

We referred earlier to the use of the *stereotype* in person perception. Since this is an important part of the process, it merits closer examination. In our general social interaction we often find that we have only one item of information about a person, such as that he is a black, a teacher or a student. In the absence of any other firm information about him, such knowledge strongly affects our perceptions. We use the term *stereotype* of the action of assigning attributes to a person solely on the basis of the class or category to which he belongs.

Brown (1965) draws an interesting distinction between *roles* and *stereotypes*:

A social role is a set of prescriptive rules, of guides to behaviour, for persons of a given category. What is prescribed for the category is ordinarily performed by the category and expected from the category. Prescription, expectancy and performance all converge in the social role, but in the social stereotype we have categorical expectancies without prescriptions and it is a matter of controversy as to whether or not the category performs in such a way as to confirm the expectancy.

In general stereotypes are indispensable to all kinds of social interaction because it is impossible to know everything about everybody. A stereotype is a kind of shorthand, a way of abstracting a number of characteristics about a person or a group to form the basis of interaction. If we had no stereotypes, interaction would become impossible because we would have to construct each encounter with a person step by step rather than by making assumptions on which interaction could proceed. Stereotypes only mislead if they lead us to make assumptions inconsistent with the types of behaviour usually shown by the kind of person with whom we are dealing. So in entering a restaurant and being approached by a waiter our stereotype tells us what we might expect of him. Our assumptions are likely to be right because the role is fairly well defined and structured. He will not bring us the sweet before the soup nor question our ability to pay, for example. Stereotypes are likely to mislead us more when we consider them as a basis for interaction with less accessible figures like hospital consultants or barristers. The television agencies have not been slow to capitalise on the relative inaccessibility of such figures by presenting their own stereotypes of them in 'soap operas'. These are often misleading because they concentrate only on the glamour of the consultant's or barrister's job and neglect the dull and repetitive aspects. Some of the stereotypes of teaching are of the same order. Teaching, as a job, tends to be presented as a subject either for comedy or for serious social comment — in both cases the dull and repetitive aspects being ignored.

Stereotypes are objectionable (as distinct from misleading) only when they force us to think of other cultural groups in terms exclusively of our own. To think of the norms of one's own group as right for all men (and, by implication, the norms of other groups as wrong) is called, in social science, *ethnocentrism*. To view and label groups thus, 'Negroes are lazy', 'Jews are mean', and imply inborn unfavourable characteristics to them is a dangerous and harmful practice, which apart from its inaccuracy and injustice has been used through recent history to justify much evil. It is the ethnic content which makes such

stereotypes objectionable and unacceptable bases for interaction, particularly in a world daily shrinking in terms of both
the cultural and the physical distance between races and ethnic
groups.

ACCURACY OF PERSON PERCEPTION

We have mentioned earlier the question of the *accuracy* of
'person perception' and obviously accuracy is crucial to the
whole process since inaccuracy, if less harmful in mere social
encounters, may be positively dangerous where professional
relations are concerned. Though it may appear that the accuracy
of 'person perception' is high in everyday life because, to
outward appearances at least, social interaction appears to work
smoothly, a large part of this smoothness can be accounted for in
terms of a general knowledge of social structure. The function
and roles of many persons in public-service occupations, such as
the waiter we discussed earlier, are so clearly defined that
knowledge of them as persons is not required. It would,
however, be possible to cultivate the friendship of a waiter in
ways beyond the strict role definition. For example, he might
also be the owner of the restaurant in which he serves. In his role
as the owner he might cash cheques for me if I were unable to get
to my bank before closing time, but favours like this are not a
part of the stated role. I could only seek such a service if my
perceptions of his reaction were accurate, otherwise I would
look and feel awkward when my request was refused.

In general the research evidence is somewhat contradictory
both as to whether accuracy is a general rather than a specific
skill and what exactly are the qualities of an accurate judge. The
study of Cline and Richards (1960) using ten colour and sound
films of interviews of ten persons covering the whole age range
from the late teens up to the mid-sixties employed fifty student
judges from a summer school (and provided therefore a more
heterogeneous sample than is usual among students). The
judging instruments included various tests of personality
characteristics and of intelligence, together with ratings of the
film sequences in the form of both overt scale measures (e.g.

trait ratings) and hidden scale measures (e.g. completing a sentence in any way a respondent wished). In general the results suggested that judging is a general skill and not a specific one. When the correlation coefficients between ratings on the first five films were compared with the remaining five films, in terms of five different judging instruments, the level obtained was reasonably high. (A correlation coefficient is a statistical index of agreement between two sets of measures ranging from $+1\cdot0$ (perfect agreement) through 0 (no agreement or disagreement) to $-1\cdot0$ (perfect disagreement).) In this case the correlation coefficients ranged from $+0\cdot66$ to $+0\cdot79$.

Cline and Richard's research is important because a further analysis of the data showed generally similar conclusions to those of another group of investigators using quite different methods (Bronfenbrenner, Harding and Gallway 1958). This conclusion was essentially that, while accuracy in perceiving people is a general ability, it can be analysed into two independent parts: *stereotype accuracy* and *differential* or *interpersonal accuracy*. Bronfenbrenner and his colleagues further brought out the important point that, while differential or interpersonal accuracy is related to sensitivity, there is an association between sensitivity and withdrawn passive attitudes. Hence interpersonal perception is sometimes not gained or acquired without hurting the perceiver. His sensitivity and skill may be bought at the cost of his own withdrawn attitudes. Hence acquiring knowledge of another is sometimes a wounding and hurtful experience, as persons acting in a counselling role, either professionally or privately, often find.

ACCURACY OF TEACHERS' PERCEPTIONS
An experimental example of how accurate teachers are in perceiving their pupils is provided by Jackson (1968).

Jackson's experiment 293 children from eleven classes at the American equivalent of British top primary or middle school range completed a forty-seven-item questionnaire about their attitudes towards school. The eleven teachers then had to predict how their pupils would respond to the questionnaire in terms of five categories ranging from 'most satisfied' to 'least satisfied'. When correlated the two sets of measures yielded a correlation coefficient of $+0.35$. This is better than the teachers picking their pupils for each category from a list at random with a pin, but only slightly better. Further analyses of the data showed that teachers could identify 'satisfied' pupils better than 'dissatisfied' ones, and estimate more accurately as to 'satisfaction' those with higher intelligence-test scores than those with lower intelligence-test scores. The investigation shows how difficult it is to tie down in a statistical manner the accuracy of perceptions in any situation where one person is perceiving a whole group of others (as in teaching). The perceptual process appears little better than chance where accuracy of perception is concerned. A word of warning, however. The teachers were doing this under the conditions previously described as those of 'being in a vacuum'. In real life the process of such perception is not 'emotion recollected in tranquillity', though under experimental conditions, such as those existing here, this form of viewing people is inevitable. It is quite possible that those teachers would have been reasonably accurate in their day-to-day dealings with pupils. To validate such accuracy, however, we would need a measure of this day-to-day performance and that would involve another experiment.

To repeat — we perceive a person as a whole though, as we have repeatedly emphasised, the whole may be split into a number of parts for analysis. As Smith (1968) notes:

What he have said about people can be said again about the way we solve a puzzle. Consider the following crypt-arithmetic puzzle:

$$\begin{array}{r} \text{SEND} \\ +\text{MORE} \\ \hline \text{MONEY} \end{array}$$

Each letter stands for a particular number from 0 to 9. The

problem is to infer the correct numbers. The theoretical system used in solving the problem concerns the arithmetic operations involved in addition. The solution is achieved when each letter has been replaced by a number and where collectively they satisfy the roles of addition. The puzzle solver begins by inspecting the pattern of letters, looking for some clue that will suggest a number for a letter. For example, in this puzzle M can only be 1. The letters are gradually replaced by numbers until we finish with

$$\begin{array}{r} 9,567 \\ +1,085 \\ \hline 10,652 \end{array}$$

As in our reactions to a person, the letters represent the initial unity that attracts and holds attention. As in our implicit theories, arithmetic allows us to find unity and meaning in the puzzle. As in our predictions about people, arithmetic allows us to make predictions concerning the numbers represented by the letters. Also, as in our predictions about people, each possible number is tested for its fit and accepted or rejected on this basis. As in our efforts to understand people, the initial unity persists throughout the solving process. Each part of the puzzle is differentiated as one discovers the correct number for each letter until finally all the letters are replaced by numbers and the puzzle is solved. Perhaps the most critical difference lies in the fact that we have one common theory of arithmetic but unnumerable theories about people.

The place of 'person perception', then, is critical in the teaching and learning process in schools though I am not sure the subject figures very prominently, if sometimes at all, either as a professional skill to be acquired or even as a substantial theoretical element in any of the teacher-training programmes in Britain known to me.

Speech and person perception

We referred earlier to the importance of the pattern of speech in both its non-linguistic and its linguistic aspects. We noted that speech formed the core of social interaction. Hence it is important to consider how the underlying structure of any social situation influences the organisation of talk. Speech patterns are both *sequential*, utterances being connected to one another in a meaningful way, and *selective*, that is the speaker selects from a number of alternatives he judges permissible and appropriate to the particular situation in which he finds himself. The 'appropriateness' of the situation we earlier called *situational* or *contextual*. Goffman (1964) puts it this way:

> Is the speaker talking to the same or opposite sex, subordinate or superordinate, one listener or many, someone right there or on the phone, is he reading a script or talking spontaneously, is the occasion formal or informal, routine or emergency?

He goes on to say:

> I would define a social situation as an environment of mutual monitoring possibilities, anywhere within which an individual will find himself accessible to the naked senses of all others who are 'present', and similarly find them accessible to him. According to this definition, a social situation arises whenever two or more individuals find themselves in one another's immediate presence, and it lasts until the next-to-last person leaves. Those in a given situation may be referred to aggregatively as a gathering, however divided, or mute and distant, or only momentarily present, the participants in the gathering appear to be. Cultural rules establish how individuals are to conduct themselves by virtue of being in a gathering, and these rules for commingling, when adhered to, socially organise the behaviour of those in the situation.

The classroom group is certainly one type of gathering in which cultural rules determine what is expected to happen, though these rules are continually changing under the influence of the wider society, and experience is necessary to assess what the current rules are. For example a child coming from a 'progressive' school will be in trouble if he addresses his new schoolmaster in a public school by his Christian name whereas formerly he may have been happy and even encouraged to do so.

The term *encounter* Goffman applies to the meeting physically of two or more persons (physically because it could be a telephone encounter) to engage by joint agreement in sustaining visual and cognitive (thinking) attention which will of course involve other senses such as hearing. There are clear rules for beginning and ending encounters, for the entrance and departure of those taking part — the participants — and jointly shared ideas between them as to the 'right' amount of space to occupy and sounds to make.

ENCOUNTERS IN THE CLASSROOM

In the classroom of course some rules are not clear and are capable of many interpretations. Teacher and pupils assemble together by some formal arrangement, e.g. the bell rings and pupils enter the school in formal or informal ways and go to their classes. They leave their classes at a prearranged signal either together, or in groups, or singly. The rules in general are clear in this respect. In other respects they are not. For example, if pupils do not work at tasks assigned to them what action does the teacher take? He is likely to ask himself some questions. Are the tasks too difficult for the pupils? Or too easy? Is there a disruptive pupil stopping the others from working? The teacher has to weigh the probabilities and work out particular rules he hopes the pupils will follow.

These rules may, for example, entail the pupils working for shorter periods than they did before, or for longer periods before coming to consult the teacher, or perhaps removing the disruptive pupil if this can be arranged, or giving more time to preparing the pupils' tasks and so on. All these activities will be designed to make the teacher's role, in achieving what he thinks the pupils should do, easier, but they will only work if pupils accept them. The acceptance by the pupils of the new rules has in fact to be *negotiated* and the negotiation aspect we have already termed *transactional*. Such negotiations involve both space and sounds, particularly the latter. The teacher may say 'Please be quiet' or 'Shut up' and may or may not give reasons for his action. His actions will be aimed at establishing between himself and the pupils ideas about the amount of noise he will tolerate. Their actions of either complying with his request or of disobeying it and hence generating more interactions will all be part of this negotiating process. The teacher is the senior partner but pupils have an important partnership function too.

The behaviours of teacher and pupils in a classroom are basically composed of a series of encounters, teacher with pupil(s) and pupil(s) with pupil(s). The classroom group is not basically a collection of what Goffman terms 'merely unengaged participants bound by unfocused interaction', though such a condition can exist for a period of time, such as when a teacher fails to meet his class on their first assembling together. Of course in a class of the *Blackboard Jungle* type Goffman's definition may describe their behaviours very accurately. Put another way, in such a class there is no *series* of focused encounters, only a number of fairly random and unfocused ones. In both cases negotiation or transaction will be involved, primarily through speech. Goffman notes:

I am suggesting that the act of speaking must always be referred to the state of talk that is sustained through the particular turn at talking, and that this state of talk involves a circle of others ratified as coparticipants. (Such a phenomenon as talking to oneself, or talking to unratified recipients as in the case of collusive communication, or telephone talk, must first be seen as a departure from the norm, else its structure and significance will be lost.) Talk is socially organised, not merely in terms of who speaks to whom in what language, but as a little system of mutually ratified and ritually governed face-to-face action, a social encounter. Once a state of talk has been ratified, cues must be available for requesting the floor and giving it up, for informing the speaker as to the stability of the focus of attention he is receiving. Intimate collaboration must be sustained to ensure that one turn at talking neither overlaps the previous one too much, nor wants for inoffensive conversational supply, for someone's turn must always and exclusively be in progress.

Now though reference is being made here to all types of social encounter, in general the classroom is, or ideally should be, distinctly organised to produce encounters with all members technically having authority (what Goffman calls 'ratified as coparticipants' in the above passage) to speak (though not all at once, of course). The teacher and pupils 'request the floor and give it up' in a particularly unique way because the teacher is arbiter both by reason of his stated or assumed role and by reason of the power that it confers on him. He can take steps to ensure 'intimate collaboration' and can ratify participants' cooperation. Or he can fail to do so partially or totally. One measure of his success in the job will be how successful he is in achieving these ends.

Utterances and gestures   Goffman notes that while the utterances of participants must be in accord with linguistic principles (that is, with the rules of grammar and syntax) these utterances have another function, namely as the basis for gestures. These gestures keep the conversation going and provide the foundation for a whole set of speech-related acts. For example, withdrawing from an encounter is invariably accompanied by a change of posture which can be further accompanied by a change of intonation of the voice or by vocal sighs. Teachers experience a lot of this type of behaviour from pupils, though they generally have neither the time nor the expertise to analyse it, as indeed do few of us in either professional or private situations. Face-to-face interactions are different in kind from either written statements or the sort of language used internally when solving problems, for example, and they have their own processes and their own structure. These processes are not essentially linguistic in character though often expressed through a linguistic medium.

PSYCHOLINGUISTIC IMPLICATIONS

In the area where psychology and linguistics meet, which is termed *psycholinguistics*, there is a frequent discrepancy between behaviour and competence, that is, between speaking and language. Traditionally in psycholinguistic theory, any interaction presupposes we have, first, theories as to whether the users are linguistically competent and in what that competence consists — the *competence theory*. Second, it presupposes that we need to construct ways of measuring how that competence is reflected, or made real, in the acts of speaking and hearing — *the performance model*.

Competence theory basically refers to the speaker–hearer's ability to generate and understand (grammatically correct) utterances. *The performance model* basically refers to his *practical ability* to do this. As Chomsky (1965) says:

> When we say that a sentence has a certain derivation with respect to a particular generative grammar, we say nothing about how the speaker or hearer might proceed, in some practical or efficient way, to construct such a derivation. These questions belong to the theory of language use — the theory of performance.

The meaning of speach, then, as far as the linguist is concerned, is fairly restricted in that it is tied to the establishment of relations and references in oral utterances through the use of formal types of reasoning. It is aimed at producing finite and 'expected' outcomes, such as we described above in terms of the sort of inner dialogue used in solving problems. While accepting the basic definitions of competence theory and the performance model, it must be said that the formal usage of speech does not simply arise from classroom experience and ability levels: a critical factor is the social relationship between the participants. As Giglioli (1972) notes, 'speech becomes understandable only in connection with social interaction.' Most people talk freely and often among others with whom they feel comfortable, taking many liberties in their style of speech, using slang terms, abbreviated words and so on (Blum and Gumperz 1971). So when the teacher says 'Please be quiet' or 'Shut up' neither the teacher's competence nor his performance, in the purely psycholinguistic terms we have described, is likely to be very satisfactory. However, if we look upon such comments as a measure or index of teacher frustration, perhaps arising in turn from his pupil's frustration, the words in fact reflecting the mutual discomfort of teacher and pupil, we may come to a better understanding of such activities as *indexes of behaviour expressed through language, but not primarily linguistic.*

A slightly lengthier and more complex view of the topic is expressed by Cicourel (1973) in describing some research involving two multiracial classes of young children in an American elementary school who had been observed over an eight-month period during which they had completed various standardised psycholinguistic, reading and intelligence tests. A major part of the research was to examine the assumptions that test constructors must make about the child's world in order to develop measures of intelligence and general knowledge. He concludes:

> The work, however, underlines the problems mentioned earlier about the child's ability to utilise perceptual experiences, or his memory of these experiences, in contexts where verbal expressions are necessary for the teacher to assess the child's ability and achievement. It becomes impossible to separate competence from performance because the linguist's and psycholinguist's models are not realistically based on the ways in which children seem to develop and display cognitive abilities that transcend language use itself. The child may be forced to process information couched in grammatically correct sentences produced by the teacher as a way of satisfying educational goals, but this does not constitute a test of how the child receives, organises and generates information nor is it a test of what he understands about the setting or

task. The teacher's utterances and intentions in combination with the use of perceptual materials for conveying a lesson may appear to be ambiguous and/or contradictory for the child. The child's ability to produce utterances recognised by the psycholinguist and teacher as grammatically adequate may not index his ability to understand the syntactic or lexical complexities the teacher or researcher produces.

What I think this final section implies for any student of the subject is that in any social interaction we need to look at the meaning both *within* and *beyond* the purely linguistic forms and the given normative and cultural rules, to variables such as speech patterns and the whole gamut of bodily and sense impressions and actions we described earlier.

3

Leadership in teaching

The nature of leadership in teaching

While teachers are often popularly supposed to be natural leaders, it is important to distinguish between leadership as an *organisational function* and leadership as a *personal quality*. Confusion about the two ends has led to all kinds of misunderstandings about teacher function. So the degree to which teachers exert or exhibit leadership depends in large measure on the characteristics of the classes with which they are involved. To attain the role of teacher will certainly entail a minimum level of 'leadership' quality and this will be a function of the personality structure of the individual. But *it is the organisational or environmental quality of the school that will largely determine how far the teacher develops, or fails to develop particular leadership qualities.*

Leadership in teaching poses rather different problems from those of leadership in other groupings of individuals. This is because the led (i.e. the pupils) are separated by age from the adult level of development and are confronted by a range of developmental tasks such as is not found in a group composed wholly of adults.

Developmental tasks   The concept of a *developmental task* was first worked out by Havighurst (1953) and might briefly be defined as the successful completion of certain learning tasks at various stages of a person's life. If successfully completed, such tasks lead to mental adjustment and provide the basis for further progress — hence the label 'developmental'. If a person fails to complete them successfully his mental adjustment is hindered and such a hindrance may lead to personal unhappiness, difficulties in relationships and difficulties in later tasks.

Pupils are in the groups we call school classes because, in the first place, parents put them there. Though this element of parental compulsion may be gradually internalised by the pupil (so that he goes to school almost of his own volition) truancy shows that the idea of compulsion can persist and, at an appropriate developmental stage, be rejected in the form of truancy, disruptive behaviour and so on.

Pupils accept control of their activities in the classroom in some measures from outside pressures ('If you don't work you won't get a good job') and in some measure from the satisfaction of the varied needs of group affiliation, such as the pleasure derived from working together with like-minded and similarly aged pupils on making a model. Both of these control factors are to an extent dependent on the quality of leadership displayed. Where the teacher is accepted, i.e. is allowed to display leadership quality, it is because he is perceived by the majority of pupils, however dimly, as satisfying those needs and pressures.

THE DERIVATION OF A TEACHER'S LEADERSHIP FUNCTION

As we have previously suggested, no teacher teaches except by consent, however much he construes the situation as being one where he imposes rules of behaviour or procedure. In the same way that the act of teaching does not guarantee the act of learning, so the desire to impose behavioural rules does not guarantee their observance. The rules and procedures of the leader (teacher) are only likely to be followed where they are thought to bring benefits to the followers (pupils). As children get older they will, on the whole, be less and less amenable to rules and procedures of which they do not see the point or benefit.

Through the act of leading, then, the leader organises the

activities of the group towards the accomplishment of some end. The teacher is not chosen as a leader by the group, as in some voluntary forms of group association. This makes the attainment of particular goals more difficult because in some degree the teacher has to impose them, whether or not the pupils' consent is readily forthcoming. When, too, those appointing the leader are themselves not of one mind as to the aims and ends of the organisation (the school) then the difficulty of leadership is quite considerable. This situation is especially true of the appointing body of a school whose views about the nature of the educational process are likely to be very varied, though those views will seldom need collective expression in practice.

So teacher is charged with leadership, not from below, from the followers (pupils), but from above. However, for the effective function of the classroom group the teacher must appear to the pupils as the means whereby their needs will be satisfied. Herein lies much of the current difficulty over classroom control and the problems of creating, at times, even minimally satisfactory conditions of learning. 'Why should I? You've no rights over me!' are now the freely expressed sentiments of some pupils. Where the actual derivation of leadership is challenged, then the whole operation of group processes is at risk and so the leader's task becomes doubly hard. He often has to strive for both the acceptance of his role as teacher and its implementation in terms of the effective learning of his pupils.

In general, the phenomenon of leadership is much more complex than the romantic concepts, the glamorous myths, that sometimes seem to attach themselves to leaders. Some of the same romantic ethos attaches to the 'born teacher' whose leadership qualities, it is often said, are the essence of his effectiveness. It is better, however, to consider leadership less romantically, and to view it as a function of the needs existing in the relationship between an individual and a group. Obviously the personality of the leader will have some part to play in such a function, though personality will not be the all-embracing factor that determines the essential quality of leadership.

While a person does not achieve leadership solely by his possessing a particular number of personality traits in combination, or by possessing a certain unique personality trait labelled 'leadership', personal characteristics obviously play a part in the individual's enactment of the role of leadership.

PERSONAL FACTORS ASSOCIATED WITH LEADERSHIP

Some early research evidence (Stogdill 1948) suggested that the following personal factors are associated with leadership:

1 *Capacity* (intelligence, alertness, verbal facility, originality, judgement).

2 *Achievement* (scholarship, knowledge, athletic accomplishments).

3 *Responsibility* (dependability, initiative, persistence, aggressiveness, self-confidence, desire to excel).

4 *Participation* (activity, sociability, cooperation, adaptability, humour).

5 *Status* (socio-economic position, popularity).

These findings are much in accord with what might be expected, and the passage of time has tended to confirm Stogdill's findings — 'a classic in social psychology' (Gibb 1969). Leadership is associated with the attainment of goals, with getting things done, and these qualities would facilitate such activity. In teaching they appear of similar importance, though the age differential between teacher and taught tends perhaps to emphasise the importance of different qualities at different stages.

For example, in the teaching of very young children the qualities of *participation* might be of higher value than *status*, whereas *capacity* might be of more value than *status* in the teaching of pupils of the sixteen-to-eighteen range preparing themselves for higher education. Obviously the pattern of personal factors will vary with the situation in which the teacher finds himself and this is perhaps the key to leadership style. By *situation* (mental level, status, skills, needs and interests of followers, objectives to be achieved etc.) is meant the social context in which the leader operates.

It has been said that effective teaching is a matter of the teacher finding the 'right' niche, i.e. the appropriate *situation* in which to operate. So, if there is a mismatch between the personal factors and the situation — such as where teachers with high academic qualifications in a subject discipline (*achievement*) were arbitrarily assigned to teach linguistically-deprived children with behaviour problems (*situation*) — effective and happy teaching relations are unlikely to prosper. In teaching, as in other spheres of professional social interaction, it is not especially difficult to find persons who are leaders. It is quite another matter, however, to place these persons in different situations where their leadership function can be exercised. In other words, *situational* factors are crucial to the exercise of leadership. As Morrison and McIntyre (1973) note in the words of one American commentator:

> The criterion is not whether the teacher exhibits or fails to exhibit a particular kind of leadership style . . . but rather whether the style he exhibits is congruent with the *leadership style established to be effective for the conditions under which he teaches* [my italics].

So a student teacher who practices his teaching in rural schools will often find such a leadership style (probably gentle and polite) inappropriate and unsuccessful if he takes up his first post in a tough inner-city area.

LEADERS AND FOLLOWERS

It is important to remember that the concept of leadership involves two persons or sets of persons — the leader and the led. The term 'leadership' is applied to the interaction arising from the two entities. Hence, while leadership qualities have been discussed in terms of the personality of the leader, little reference has yet been made to those he leads — his followers. We can think, then, of the bonds between them as follows:

1 Each person perceives the other as a leader or as a follower.
2 Each person already has, or develops, an aversion or a

liking for the other.

3 Each person proceeds to integrate these two viewpoints which can be described as the integration of cognitive and emotional elements.

In considering the relation of teacher and pupil it can be seen that, depending on the age and the developmental level of the pupil, the teacher is likely to be viewed more emotionally than cognitively in his leadership function by young children; and, conversely, cognitive perceptions will operate more forcibly with older children. A similar matching set of perceptions will in all probability operate on the part of the teacher towards his pupils, though when they do not the conditions could be fruitful for generating the typical pupil-behaviour problems that can occur. Many of these problems arise because the *interaction process* is not working smoothly. If one or both parties seek differing degrees of reward (or need satisfaction) in cognitive and/or emotional elements simultaneously, then conflict inevitably ensues.

This poses the problem of the nature of teaching. If the term leadership is an abstraction that refers to a special kind of social expectation, then it can be seen that teachers' expectations of pupils and pupils' expectations of teachers are difficult to align consistently. Conflict is endemic in teaching, because while it is at first sight a type of *push* leadership it is, on closer examination, a *pull* type also. These terms are outlined in detail in Cooper and McGough (1963).

PUSH AND PULL LEADERSHIP

Push leadership is the *dominance–submissive* type of relationship, common among animal species, where certain members of a colony or group are of higher status than the others and impose their behavioural desires on others. Such relations are characterised by 'pecking orders' which is a particular term used in describing the hierarchical behaviour among species of birds. *Pull* leadership, on the other hand, is characterised by certain group members initiating activity that other members copy without apparent coercion. So amongst certain species of birds their migratory progress is characterised by one bird or a small group of birds leading the rest of the flock.

The social behaviour of humans is, of course, often a combination of the two kinds, and teaching is particularly so. The conflict between the two kinds can be seen in the teacher's insistence on behavioural rules — 'push' leadership ('Do this! Do it this way!') — coupled with his desire to engage and stretch his pupils — 'pull' leadership ('Now I am going to show you . . . If you do it this way . . .').

To apply the principles of animal behaviour directly to human intercourse is, however, only to comprehend a part of the complex pattern of such interaction. It is particularly important in this regard to emphasise the ego-conservation nature of man. He constructs all his activities (whether they actually happen as others state, or happen in the way he perceives and describes them does not matter) to protect his own self-concept or self-image and his own mental equilibrium. In so doing he is aided by the varied nature of human language, perception and cognition. These capacities in greater or lesser degree enable him to organise his mental structures so as to interpret 'pull' leadership as 'push' leadership and vice versa, to be outwardly dominated while inwardly planning to succeed to the leadership role when favourable circumstances present themselves, or, at the other extreme, to be outwardly dominating while inwardly uncertain, and so on. The variety of responses is enormous and hence the predictability of particular behaviours is almost impossible.

Effective leadership in teaching

The difficulty of teaching is that because these aspirant-leader behaviours are hard to analyse and even harder to predict, and because the developmental differences between the two parties, teacher and taught, are fixed by the difference in their chronological ages, a tremendous element of uncertainty has to be tolerated if the relationship is not to become either humdrum or bellicose. That relations between the two parties are often no worse than they are can be attributed to two things. First, to the *consensus phenomenon*, which is a tacit agreement between the two parties to take their conflicts only to a certain mutually agreed stage. Second, to the fact that each supposes he knows the *behavioural expectations* of the other, i.e. how in any future situation the other is going to act and react. He may not in reality know the other's behavioural expectations but the expectation is often enough to control the other's behaviour. In essence tolerance of ambiguity and uncertainty is the hallmark of effective leadership in teaching.

A leader must have followers, for without followers the label 'leader' is meaningless. Similarly a teacher has pupils. Further, teachers need the consent of pupils to exercise their role, i.e. to teach. The cultural ambience of the first half of the twentieth century, when consent was not considered an issue in teaching, should not disguise the reality that the consent was often as lacking then as it appears to be now, but showed itself less in disruptive antisocial behaviour and more in withdrawn and sullen behaviours. Now the pupil sometimes strikes (objects or people) rather than sulks. That this consent is no longer automatic should surprise no student of either psychology or social trends. The advocates of 'pupil power' have only made explicit in the second half of the century, under the influence of changing social customs, what was already implicit, namely the power of followers to influence leaders. When those leaders cannot, by the nature of their function, be chosen by their followers and when they occupy a particularly separate position by reason of age, then pupils may challenge the teacher's authority.

INFLUENCE OF SUBORDINATES
Warr and Wall (1975) in discussing leadership in organisations generally note that, even at the adult level, it is quite possible 'that subordinate attitudes determine leadership style rather than the reverse.' They quote the study of Lowin and Craig (1968) who arranged for forty-eight people to be hired for supervising office work. Twenty-four were given subordinates

who deliberately performed poorly. Twenty-four were given subordinates who performed well. The closeness of supervision and the degree of consideration of the forty-eight were monitored. Supervisors with 'poor' subordinates adopted closer, more structured and less considerate leadership styles than those with 'good' subordinates. Warr and Wall conclude: 'the pattern is almost bound to be one of mutual influence — leaders affecting subordinates, and subordinates affecting leaders.'

In teaching, then, there is a greater gap between leadership and followership than is found in most other groups. Perhaps the words of Gibb (1954) are of relevance in describing the peculiar difficulties of teachers:

> Followers subordinate themselves, not to *an individual whom they perceive as utterly different*, but to a member of their group who has superiority at this time and *who they perceive to be fundamentally the same as they are* [my italics].

Perhaps some of the problems arising in school classrooms in the behavioural sphere occur because pupils do not perceive the teacher to be fundamentally the same as they are. The status gap is very wide and is not completely bridged by informality on the teacher's part, though this may help. By *status* here is meant Hollander's (1964) description of the term as *the placement of an individual along a dimension, or in a hierarchy, by virtue of some criterion of value.* Here again reference is being made to the situational nature of leadership because the 'status' describes the perception of each party by the other, the interpersonal perception of the teacher by the pupil and vice versa, where the behaviour of the teacher is not just seen by itself but is matched against the expectations of the pupil.

In considering the leader–follower issue when applied to teaching, however, it is important to stress that age and developmental differences do not preclude, in many cases, the operation of the normal conventions of group behaviour. They only serve to illustrate that such differences are more fixed and more institutionalised than in almost any other human group.

NELSON'S EXPERIMENT

The problem of demonstrating empirically the similarities and differences among leaders and followers with respect to teachers and pupils arises from the fact that the majority of experimental studies of followership involve adult groups where the status gap is nothing like as wide as in teacher–pupil groups. However, an experimental study by Nelson (1964) of four approximately equal groups of Arctic scientists living together over a winter is fairly relevant. Each group contained between seventeen and nineteen scientists. The attitudinal and behavioural characteristics of the seventy-two scientists were evaluated by two independent supervisors, and, by splitting the groups on scales of 'leadership' and 'likeability', four groups of 'liked' and 'less-liked' leaders and followers were obtained. As might have been expected, both 'liked' and 'less-liked' leaders exhibited more self-confident and aggressive behaviours than comparable groups of followers. But there were some similarities in attitudes to teamwork and respect for forms of authority between 'liked' leaders and 'liked' followers — more so than between 'liked' leaders and 'less-liked' leaders, between 'liked' followers and 'less-liked' followers, and between 'less-liked' leaders and 'less-liked' followers.

The findings could give a clue as to the type of relations that can operate between teacher and taught, even given the status differentials already referred to. 'Liking' for his pupils is not the sole criterion on which any teacher can operate, since he is charged with the welfare of all pupils (another critical difference between the classroom and other groups). However, such preferences, as revealed in Nelson's experiment, for positive attitudes to teamwork and respect for forms of authority obviously commend themselves to teachers as a basis for preferring pupils with such qualities over others because these qualities aid group functioning. Therefore the phenomenon of 'favouritism' so despised (perhaps rightly) by pupils often has its basis, not in the whimsical preference of the teacher for a particular pupil but in the added control function which it might confer on the teacher. Of course most teachers will not have analysed the matter in this way, and 'favouritism' produces its own difficulties in the longer term, but it is an understandable stance to employ and few people in any controlling or supervisory role will be completely free of its use.

PUPIL CONTRIBUTIONS TO GROUP LEARNING

It was suggested earlier that teachers could be both leaders and followers given appropriate circumstances, and certainly the effective teacher needs to be aware of, and to practise, the art of 'giving his pupil his head' if creative learning is to be encouraged. Since learning proceeds from both imitation of and identification with others, as well as from direct instruction or demonstration, the contribution of pupils to learning can be of virtually equal importance to that of the teacher. This is not always perceived to be so, however, by either observers of the group or participants in it.

In any group some members make contributions that are more important and more indispensable than those of other members. Some help the group achieve its objectives in one way, some in another. At times, especially in captive groups like schoolchildren ('captive' in the sense earlier referred to of not freely choosing to be members, but being compelled so to be), members may consciously or unconsciously oppose, hinder the achievement of, or even reject the means of helping the group achieve its objectives. But, given that the concern here is with leader-like behaviour, then in terms of these definitions the essence of such behaviour is that it aids the achievement of group objectives.

It is not, then, specific behaviours that mark out leaders but rather a leader's particular relationships with other group members. Where these relationships help group functioning they are leader-like qualities; where they impede or retard it they are not. It was suggested earlier that while certain personal factors are associated with the exercise of effective leadership there was no one 'leadership quality' that marked out leaders from their fellows. In fact different kinds of groups need different leaders or facilitators and even within the same group different people may assume the leadership role and perform equally well in it. This also leads one to question whether the *named* leader is always the *actual* leader — for example, the distinction that the law draws between *de jure* (by right) and *de facto* (in fact) is apposite here.

TASK ACHIEVEMENT AND SOCIO-EMOTIONAL NEEDS

Bales (1958) has drawn attention to the important phenomenon of distinguishing between those people who are good facilitators, or leaders, in regard to ensuring that a group achieves the tasks assigned to it (tasks either assigned by outside agencies or inspired by members), and those leaders who satisfy the personal needs of members, in relation both to the task and to each other. The distinction is essentially between *task achievement* and *socio-emotional* needs and many leaders are not equally proficient in both spheres. Hence leadership roles can swing back and forth between two or more persons while the whole group process is in operation.

Bales's experiment with four five-man groups over twelve sessions clearly indicates how, after the first session, the relationship between the production of good ideas and being liked tends to be an inverse one. That is to say that the more good ideas a group member produces the less he tends to be liked. Bales's own words may be the best comment available on his findings:

> Could it be that there was something about arriving in a top-status position, owing to technical contributions to the task problems of the group, that tended to 'lose friends and alienate people'? If so, was another man likely to arise who paid more attention to the social-emotional problems of the group and so tended to collect more liking? The idea that this happens with sufficient frequency that it can be viewed as typical may be called 'the hypothesis of two complementary leaders'.

It is perhaps important to emphasise that a group member who does not produce any good ideas can be disliked as well. Bales's evidence suggests only that the mooting of good ideas is one likely way of incurring dislike. There are of course other ways of incurring dislike. In the experimental context, however, the smallness of the groups probably did not allow much scope for this kind of decision to develop, whereas in a larger group in real life it might well do so.

This obviously has applicability to teaching because, while the teacher ought ideally to be capable of satisfying both *task achievement* and *socio-emotional* needs, the age differential, and the consequences that flow from it, may emphasise his role as task achiever. The other needs that any group has — and classroom groups are no exception — could be satisfied by another person or persons, in this case the pupils. So it is not fanciful to suggest again that the teacher can be a leader one moment and a follower the next in the circumstances that have been described. There can of course be occasions when the teacher is apparently 'in command', and catering for all the group's needs all the time, but closer examination will often reveal that the appearance is deceptive.

Multiplying effect   Gibb (1969) comments upon Kahn and Katz's (1960) studying of the relationship between working groups and their supervisors and, while the study itself has limited relevance for teaching, the consequences that flow from it are relevant. The problem is the one we noted earlier, namely, that the term 'productivity' used in this and similar studies is not wholly appropriate to schools.

Kahn and Katz's study was concerned with the differences of supervising behaviour in groups with 'high' and 'low' production achievement, which can be a function of either the technical skill of the leader (that is, he demonstrates how a job can be done and group members imitate him) or his ability to motivate members to use the group's resources to the full. In so far as the leader can stimulate others to use their resources more fully he has, so to speak a *multiplying effect* which may be more significant to the group's functioning than just technical skill.

This multiplying effect refers at root to a person's ability to increase the skill or the performance of another group member, who may in turn increase another member's skill and so on, the effect of one being multiplied throughout the group. As we have said, such an effect does not necessarily stem from technical know-how, planning or coordinating skills on the supervisor's part, but can stem equally from the supportive and encouraging attitudes that a supervisor exhibits. This is somewhat akin to Bales's distinction between the two types of group needs and, inevitably, will not always lie with the official leader of the group.

One aspect that such studies in industry and commerce have illustrated is that the *official* leader is not always the man or woman who exerts or appears to exert the most influence. Such influence can come from other group members working behind the scenes. In some cases an apparently 'weak' leader, by working inconspicuously, makes and implements important decisions. Conversely a 'strong' leader may make a high verbal impact but fail to inspire group members or implement any sizeable decisions.

Leadership styles in teaching

It is probably important to regard the quality of leadership as one of degree, rather than as an 'all or none' affair. Sometimes it is exercised publicly, sometimes privately. Sometimes it is seen to be ascendant; sometimes it appears absent or negative or negatived by group members. Of no quality is the phrase 'You can't win them all' more apt than of leadership. Popular fiction and journalism often convey the false impression of the leader winning, persuading, controlling everyone. This image does not correspond with the reality, which is that the leader has to alternate in dominance with other members of the group according to their needs, desires and whims, though he may hold the titular role of leader.

Teaching often appears to reward, both in the long-term financial sense and in the immediate 'control' sense, the 'strong' leader, that is the one who gives direction, assumes an air of command and usually talks a lot. This situation is inevitable, given that teaching is largely an exchange of which the spoken word is the principal currency. The difficulty we have already noted of applying the 'production' model to teaching, a difficulty that will not inhibit us from returning several more times to it, lies in this excess of verbal interaction. Teaching effectiveness often seems to be evaluated in a popular sense by the excess number of words spoken by the teacher relative to the pupil. Theoretically this excess is often deplored as educationally unsound when its existence is experimentally demonstrated (Flanders 1967 and 1970), but firm and strong verbal control still appears to be the leadership norm by which 'good' teachers are all too often popularly described. This is not to suggest that such norms are the sole models by which teachers are known, since 'strong' verbal leadership is not nowadays so universally approved as it once was. Hence other forms and approaches are also in evidence, such as a gentle, quieter approach using the pupils' verbal contributions skilfully, an approach termed by Flanders 'indirect influence'. However, few teachers will occupy the role previously described of the 'weak' leader working inconspicuously behind the scenes towards effective decision making. If teachers appear 'weak' they are more than likely to *be* weak.

By reason of the developmental differences between teachers and pupils, teachers are likely to have a tendency to adopt a 'strong' leadership style with a large oral element. While certain groups of children, such as maladjusted pupils with special behavioural difficulties, may require different teaching approaches if their problems are to be alleviated, the cultural influences, particularly those of the British milieu, place a premium on the authoritative, directive approach which is likely to operate with many groups of pupils.

Teachers, too, while they were pupils themselves were almost certainly brought up in the main under 'strong' leadership. Even the very existence of delinquent or deviant groups may sometimes be said (quite wrongly one feels) to be associated with 'weak' leadership styles, and so tends to confirm the success of the 'strong' leadership styles.

CONSIDERATION AND INITIATING STRUCTURE

Perhaps one of the most comprehensive empirical investigations into the nature of leadership behaviour was undertaken at Ohio State University in the fifties and is reported by Fleishman (1973). Using a variety of experimental techniques such as personal interviews, written questionnaires, observation and abstracting definitions from manuals of organisational processes, experts derived some 1,800 statements about leadership behaviour. By eliminating those that overlapped and duplicated one another, 150 statements were derived, which were arranged in questionnaire form and completed by large numbers of industrial and military personnel. By complex statistical techniques two dimensions were revealed that describe, in virtually all cases, the nature of leadership behaviour. These were called *consideration* and *initiating structure. Consideration* involves human qualities such as warmth, respect, empathy and approachability, and corresponds to our earlier description of a group's 'socio-emotional needs'. *Initiating structure* refers to the organisational nature of the leader's behaviour, such as defining the roles of subordinates to seniors and vice versa, and the development of patterns for achieving the group's goals or objectives. It corresponds to our earlier description of a group's 'task-achievement' function.

Three leadership styles   Getzels and Guba (1957) suggested how school leadership could be described somewhat parallel to the above, in terms of three kinds of leadership:

1 The *nomothetic leader* who is keen to stress the institution's requirements and judges staff on how they keep to fixed rules and procedures. This corresponds to 'initiating structure'.

2 The *ideographic leader* who places more emphasis on the individual needs of staff and seeks more personal relations with them, relying on staff members' own judgements rather than fixed rules. This corresponds to 'consideration'.

3 The *transactional leader* who balances the two previous approaches, trying to cater both for institutional requirements and the individual needs of staff.

The authors suggest that the transactional leader is likely to be most effective. In passing, it is perhaps important to note that, while Getzels and Guba are primarily concerned with heads of schools, their comments can apply equally well to class teachers, who will have the same options open to them of adopting one of the defined leadership styles.

FACILITATIVE BEHAVIOURS AND PSYCHOLOGICAL DISTANCE

Newcomb, Turner and Converse (1965) note that the facilitative behaviours exercised by group members, and which a leader ideally should possess in abundance, include the following:

1 Providing warmth, friendliness.

2 Conciliating, resolving conflict, relieving tension.

3 Providing personal help, counsel, encouragement.

4 Showing understanding, tolerance of different points of view.

5 Showing fairness, impartiality.

Though this seems a sweet and reasonable prescription for all types of groups, the problem that arises when we consider the position of a formal leader is very real. How can a leader be both *assessor* (the formal or task-achievement role) and *friend* (the informal, catering-for-social-needs role)? How can he both tell the same people off one minute and be friendly towards them the next? The authors quote Fiedler's research (1960) in this connection in which he examined a number of groups (school basketball teams, student survey teams, shift workers in open-hearth steel mills) and consistently found that the 'more effective' leaders were less friendly towards their fellow members, and more concerned with the task in hand than 'less effective' ones. This phenomenon is labelled *psychological distance* (or sometimes *social distance*). Effective leaders tend to keep group members 'at a distance' in all their relations with them and do not become 'one of the boys'; ineffective leaders tend to exhibit opposite behaviours. Where the group is fairly like-minded, or in technical terms 'cohesive', then these stances are in general quite acceptable to group members.

The application of such principles to teaching is a complex matter. Certainly teachers are likely to act in the general direction of points 1-5 above in regard to their pupils, since such behaviours assist group cohesiveness and hence should assist the learning process. However, teachers too have an assessment role, a task-achievement function and this, coupled with the age differentials, makes the issues less clear than they might otherwise be. Where pupils are either closer to the teacher's age level and academically inclined (e.g. pre-entrants to higher education aged from sixteen and nineteen years), or far removed and largely at the social stage of development (e.g. children first entering school at five years), then the teacher is likely to be able to cater for the socio-emotional needs of the group more easily, because his task-achievement needs in an academic sense will either be minimal (as with infant children), or fairly readily accepted (as with the pre-entrants to higher education), and the 'psychological distance' aspect will virtually take care of itself.

In children between the ages of eight and sixteen years, however, the task itself is likely to be somewhat ambiguous, because not all such children will be of the same mind as the teacher concerning their academic future. Hence his primary task achievement — getting them to learn — will often be an area of conflict in itself and the consideration of socio-emotional needs will take second place. The experimental evidence, which has already been discussed, has tended to emphasise that the acceptability of 'psychological distance' in the groups concerned arose, in part, because such groups were on the small side and leaders tended to be chosen by the prior agreement of the group members themselves. In a sense the two groups we discussed at first (sixteen- to nineteen and five-year-olds), in which conflict is likely to be minimal, correspond in some degree to the experimental groups. The older, 'academic' pupils may have exercised some choice of their teacher as much for his personal qualities as for his subject, and the groups are likely to be smaller than among the younger age ranges of pupil. As far as the five-year-olds are concerned they will have had little experience of other teachers. So their placement with a particular teacher may appear to the child to have many of the elements of choice, given the absence of what the concepts 'choice' or 'no choice' really mean.

CONFLICT AND UNCERTAINTY IN PUPILS

It is only when the distance between the leader and the led is at its greatest that doubts as to the leadership role may arise on both sides. In a sense this appreciation of distance comes with the developing complexity of both genetic and environmental influences on the child, and when he has emerged from the infant stage. The school system appears to direct him here, there and everywhere, and conflict to a greater or lesser degree, however balanced a person he may be, is inevitable. Task achievement in the form of academic prowess, then, particularly across the age band of from eight to sixteen years of age, remains on the whole the dominant concern of schools and society. The school or teacher that takes a primarily socio-emotional line at the expense of academic interests tends to be seen as deviant. Such schools or teachers who appear to have encouraged excessive friendliness and informality in any overt manner below the statutory school-leaving age are often the subject of inquiry and/or comment at either the official or the informal level. This is a complex matter extending far beyond the bounds of any analysis of group behaviour, and having sociological, economic, philosophic and political considerations out of place here. Suffice it to say that in our culture task achievement is generally seen as a matter of first importance in schools — task achievement meaning, in our cultural context, academic task achievement. In general, the socio-emotional needs are seen as complementary to task achievement. There are some exceptions of course, such as the case of severely maladjusted children, where it is perhaps conceded that catering for their socio-emotional needs is an adequate form of task achievement in itself, but such approbation is unlikely to be forthcoming in the case of normal pupils and there is, of course, no reason why it should be.

Achieved power and formal power

Perhaps some of these considerations about leaders arise because certain kinds of leadership are associated with the exercise of power. Leaders tend to be powerful either in the *achieved* or *formal* sense. *Achieved* power arises because the qualities of leadership a leader displays gradually incline his followers to make his suggestions, directions or dictates their own — what is technically called *internalising* them. *Formal* power is the power conferred on an individual by some agency outside the group he is charged with leading, and the role of teacher is a good example of such formal power. Of course this distinction is not a mutually exclusive one. The 'formal power' leader has still to achieve power, though the 'formal' label is likely to assist the process. Such a leader will still have to take account of the feelings, abilities and needs of group members if he is to achieve the objectives of the group, but the formal designation confers advantages on him from the start. The 'achieved power' leader on the other hand has no given 'formal' status but has to work up group feelings, loyalties etc. from scratch. Nevertheless, as success comes, he is likely to assume more and more 'formal' status and eventually perhaps be accorded such by others outside the group.

In either case the authority of the leader will come from the power that is given him by the group in their support of him. In fact the leader derives his basic authority from the group's assent to his leadership behaviour — even though this assent may not be formally expressed, or indeed in the case of one or two members may be totally lacking. It is the majority view here that counts, and should the number of members not giving their assent rise, the leader risks the loss of his authority and often, following this, his position as leader — formal or informal. Basically the power of the leader lies in his potential to exert influence on the members of his group.

THE CONTROL OF RESOURCES
The control of resources is another foundation of a leader's power. Either by allocating or withholding resources a leader exerts a profound influence. These resources may be of materials, equipment or, particularly in some areas, information. The latter is an important form of control, since many social and learning groups are constituted solely on the basis of ideas and their exchange. When information necessary to the group's functioning is withheld, then group action and inter-action is correspondingly inhibited. In more complex organisa-tions the very function of being in a position to control information is often enough to confer 'formal' leadership on the person so exercising such a function.

Power in teaching　In teaching terms the position of power thus described is very important indeed. Teachers have 'formal' power, such power being implied by the term 'teacher' itself. The natural differences between teacher and pupil to which reference has been made, the differences that arise from the developmental and age differences, are reinforced by the label 'teacher'. Over the past decade, however, it has come to be more and more realised that effective teaching (taking effective teaching as being teacher activity that results in the pupils' learning) is in large measure dependent on 'achieved' power and that the label by itself does not aid effectiveness very much. Indeed in certain social climates it hinders it. (We shall deal later with the whole question of social climate.) The teacher, then, is in a paradoxical sense both an advocate and a victim of the changing scene — he is charged with exercising 'formal' power but has to attain authority by 'achieved' power. As 'achieved' power succeeds — so his 'formal' power is confirmed. As 'achieved' power fails to succeed — so his 'formal' power is eroded and finally rejected. The phenomenon of the rebel leader who becomes an established figure is another practical illustra-tion of the move from 'achieved' to 'formal' power.

It is also in terms of resource control that teachers exercise some of their power. By denying, or acceding to, requests for classroom and school resources, pupils' behaviour individually or collectively will be affected. Such actions as giving pupils permission to go to the school library for 'free' reading when others are engaged in mathematics work, for example, or the denying of a class's favourite lesson (e.g. reading them a story) if certain behaviours are persisted in (e.g. talking), are two examples from among many that could be quoted.

The informational network is similarly important in this connection. Since most pupils are keen to know how and where they stand in relation to each other and to adults, the leader becomes for them a source of valuable information concerning themselves. Even pupils indulging in apparently antisocial and disruptive behaviour may still seek this information in spite of, and sometimes because of, their attitudes. The nature of favouritism, to which reference was earlier made, is often of the 'excess of information' type where teachers impart more information to favourite pupils — either about the pupils themselves, or about particular subject matter. This action can often be a fairly innocent ploy on the teacher's part but one that is not perceived so innocently by the pupils.

VISIBILITY

Newcomb, Turner and Converse (1965) speak of the *visibility* of group leaders. They go on to speak about the fact of this visibility making the leader a symbol of the group both internally and externally, which in turn may make the leader more sought after and gives him even more opportunities of leading others, and of being a model for others. This leads to the multiplying effects already discussed. So as the leader becomes more visible effectiveness may be multiplied, but similarly should he become less visible so may ineffectiveness.

Teachers are invariably likely to be *visible* leaders. Both the formal label and the processes already described make for this. They will therefore be *symbols* of the group particularly to outsiders, such as parents, who will speak of 'Miss X's class' rather than 'Form 4' or whatever. Being *symbols* they will also be *models* both for their pupils and, to a lesser but not insignificant degree, to outsiders such as parents or future pupils. These characteristics will tend to operate no matter how 'good' or 'bad' as teachers others may evaluate them, the 'others' being internal adults (e.g. headteachers or colleagues) or external adults (e.g. parents or school inspectors). But as models they will vary in effectiveness, and their leadership qualities will be both multiplied and reduced according to their evaluation by the others — internal or external.

INCONSISTENCY OF LEADERSHIP STYLES

Such evaluation of leaders is notoriously unreliable and hence the multiplying phenomenon is never constant — sometimes increasing, at other times decreasing. This inconsistency is noticeable in all leadership styles, since at one time a particular leader seems more favoured than another. Later, he often has to give way to someone else, only to return again to notice at a future date or remain in obscurity. This is a fairly important point. Leaders of all kinds fluctuate in both group members' and outsiders' esteem depending on circumstances, and it could be said that some 'work themselves out' (in the way that some creative artists do) and conceive a distaste for, or even a sheer inability to cope with, leadership. Some leaders hang on to their formal roles long after they have ceased to deserve the appellation of 'leader' — perhaps because our society does not allow them to retire gracefully in terms of proper financial provision.

This state described here has much applicability to teaching. Teachers vary in the esteem in which they are held by others, and some may 'work themselves out' in the way it was suggested any leader can do. While often holding on to the shadow of the role of teacher, the substance of the role may escape the holder, whose total performance is devoted to anything but achieved power. This can be seen in the attitude of older teachers in 'hanging on for one's pension' when they have long ceased to internalise a particular role, but carry out the function without personal commitment or much interest. Younger teachers in such a situation will often leave the job altogether for something else. This type of behaviour is not, of course, confined to teaching but afflicts many occupational roles. Where leadership behaviour is involved, however, as in teaching, such non-alignment of internal interest in the job often leads to a painful conflict between the teacher and his pupils and also between the teacher and his senior colleagues. (The position can be even worse where headteachers lose both the capacity and the desire for leadership.) In a sense society has not as yet caught up with the psychological phenomenon of 'working oneself out' — which phenomenon can be both internally or externally created. An internally created example would be where an individual's personality changes, often an age-related circumstance, make leadership personally intolerable. An externally created example would be where changing social circumstances make certain leadership styles innappropriate and unsuccessful and where these are seen so to be by the leader. Where a teacher, for example, of the old school of 'pupils have talk from the teacher, blackboard illustrations, write copiously and do as they're told' is confronted by pupils who won't do any of these things without showing resistance at every turn, and making group interaction virtually impossible, he may or may not feel able to adapt his style to cope with the circumstances. If he feels unable to change, it may be because of inherited factors on the teacher's part, whereby his personality responses consist of the same fixed set of responses to circumstances — any circumstances. It may arise because, though he sees change is necessary, the effort would be intolerable and damaging to his inner equilibrium. It may arise because, though he dimly perceives that something is wrong with the class's general behaviour, that is, with the interactional process of the group, he doesn't really know what it is. Or, finally, he may not even be aware that anything is wrong at all. All these behaviours can be signs that he is 'worked out' and though the first example given, arising from internal forces, was a fairly stark one to illustrate the point, such behaviours are not necessarily altogether linked with age but can assail individuals at varying parts of their working life.

The teacher as leader

The label of 'teacher', while conferring a formal leadership role on the individual, does not in itself necessarily guarantee the effective exercise of that role for all of the individual's teaching life. Because teaching takes place in a social context a teacher, to survive, has to adapt to that context. Such adaptation generally needs a conscious effort within the person to change, or more technically, *reorientate* his perceptions of people and the rules governing their behaviour. The teacher of the old school that we described above, for example, could not change his perceptions and adapt himself to the prevailing social context. Hence his difficulties with his pupils. In summary, then:

> Leadership is a type of interaction among or between people — whereby individuals influence the behaviour or motivation of others. This type of influence usually occurs within the structure of a social system and tends to contribute to its stability. Leadership refers to the attributes of a position in the social structure, the characteristics of a person, and a category of behaviour. (Lindgren 1969)

The concept of leadership in teaching, as elsewhere, tends currently to be played down because it denotes in our culture, by and large, dominance or force. The prevalence of democratic ideals in society, where participation is seen as the key to acceptable group behaviour, has emphasised the role of leading rather than directing. Nevertheless at some point in the encounter the leader has to direct and influence a group to act in one way rather than another. This issue cannot be dodged, though the recognition of this reality is often avoided in books on teaching by calling such teaching acts 'teaching procedures', 'learning practices', 'initiating behaviours' and so on.

LEWIN, LIPPITT AND WHITE'S EXPERIMENT

Some confusion in this matter of direction has of course arisen from the classic experiment often quoted (and misquoted) in the literature of Lewin, Lippitt and White (1939). They studied three different types of adult leadership styles exercised on four groups of eleven-year-old-boys, each group being subjected to (1) an 'authoritarian' regime in which the leader ordered them about and told them what to do, (2) a 'democratic' regime in which he consulted them and discussed their problems with them and (3) a *laissez-faire* regime where the leader left them to their own devices, giving them no direction or advice.

The general conclusions were, not surprisingly, that boys worked best under the 'democratic' regimes, displaying tendencies of either rebellion or apathy or cowed submission under the other two. But commentators, if not the experimenters themselves, appear to have given birth to the widespread myth that because the 'democratic' regime worked best, and 'democratic' is not 'authoritarian', 'democratic' leadership can be exercised with *authority*. The confusion is remarkable but it has persisted — gathering momentum as only facile error can. The earlier part of this chapter has been at pains to dispel that illusion, because this example is a very good indication of how the findings of psychology may be a positive hindrance to educational practice if they are misinterpreted and misapplied. The distinction the authors drew between the different leadership styles is, of course, valuable. But again it is amazing that so much precept for practice has been built on a small-scale study in which boys were the only group participants. Girls' attitudes would almost certainly have been somewhat different then (in the 1930s) and certainly now, and perhaps mixed groups (boys and girls) — the normal social learning unit of society — different again.

CHARISMATIC LEADERSHIP

Related to the leadership question in general is the idea of the 'born teacher' that leads us to consider the notion of *charismatic* leadership, which may or may not flourish in democratic climates. ('Born teacher' is the concept, certainly current in the earlier part of this century, and which still persists, albeit less strongly, that certain individuals are born with the gifts of teaching and need little if any training to teach.) *Charisma* is a Greek term that is used of a gift granted by God, enabling the recipient to have some special power over his fellow men, such as the ability to heal or to perform miracles. It was first introduced into social science by Weber (1947), who used it to describe leaders who appealed strongly to the emotions of their followers. The fading of the 'born teacher' idea is well illustrated in Hoffer's (1951) description of such a leader's followers as 'true believers' whose blind faith is based on a belief in their own worthlessness and inadequacy. In present-day democratic Western societies, where the individual's worth and adequacy are strongly recognised, the need for such a leader is obviously not felt to any great extent. Pupils reflect the norms of the wider society and hence they too feel little need for such leadership. An exception is likely to be pupils with learning or behavioural difficulties, who may feel particular inadequacies and worthlessness in themselves. It is then no accident that many teachers in this 'special education' sphere tend to be more charismatic individuals than other teachers, since only there can such approaches have full rein. It is of course a debatable point as to whether 'special education' brings out the latent charismatic approach in the teacher, or whether the charismatic nature of the teacher impelled him to choose to work there in the first place. This example poses clearly the dilemma earlier discussed as to whether leadership is a question of 'leader style' or 'the differential contexts' in which it may be exercised (Hollander and Julian 1968).

CONFRONTATION IN TEACHING

Finally, then, leadership in teaching has both similarities to, and differences from, other leadership situations. Its similarities arise from the leadership needs common to any group, its dissimilarities from the age and related developmental differences between the leader and the led, that is between a teacher and his pupils. Perhaps, however, the crucial difference between classroom groups and practically all the other groups in society is that children are there basically by force of law rather than free choice. (That some break the law by truancy, by 'voting with their feet', does not invalidate the point.) The other agencies that enforce attendance by law are prisons, the armed forces (in countries with compulsory service) and psychiatric hospitals (where certain patients are committed by court order). This particular social context, then, in which teaching takes place does not mean it is punishment and repression all the way, but that the element of the force of law is a much deeper element affecting behaviour than many social science and educational texts have, as yet, apparently and visibly recognised. Over forty years ago Waller (1965) put the issues as they have essentially remained (notwithstanding the progressive and democratic tendencies in institutional behaviour since then):

> Teacher and pupil confront each other with attitudes from which the underlying hostility can never be altogether removed. Pupils are the material in which teachers are supposed to produce results. Pupils are human beings striving to realize themselves in their own spontaneous manner, striving to produce their own results in their own way. Each of these hostile parties stands in the way of the other; in so far as the aims of either are realized, it is at the sacrifice of the aims of the other.
>
> Authority is on the side of the teacher. The teacher nearly always wins. In fact, he must win, or he cannot remain a teacher.

Though the argument is seldom posed as brutally as Waller poses it, the confrontation aspect places the leadership element in teaching in a basically different class from most other forms of institutional behaviour, and some of these elements have formed the substance of what has been said in this chapter.

4

Communication, social learning and control in teaching

Communication difficulties in teaching

A cynic once described the teaching process as 'casting false pearls before real swine' and to anyone who has done any teaching at school level and across the ability ranges (and sometimes in higher/further education also) these words carry a ring of truth that must accord at times with their thoughts in private, if not in public. That is not to say that teaching children is an unpleasant activity, only that communicating with them can, at times, be extremely difficult and wearing, as any teacher or parent will know. One pertinent paper in the literature (Bauer 1964) begins its title with the words 'The Obstinate Audience', and though the paper is concerned with communication in both group face-to-face experiments and among wider audiences (e.g. as in advertising) one of its quotations, namely that of Davison (1959), is very relevant to teaching:

... the communicator's audience is not a passive recipient — it cannot be regarded as a lump of clay to be moulded by the master propagandist. Rather, the audience is made up of individuals who demand something from the communications to which they are exposed, and who select those that are likely to be useful to them. In other words, they must get something from the manipulator if he is to get something from them. A bargain is involved. Sometimes, it is true, the manipulator is able to lead his audience into a bad bargain by emphasising one need at the expense of another or by representing a change in the significant environment as greater than it actually has been. But audiences, too, can drive a hard bargain. Many communicators who have been widely disregarded or misunderstood know that to their cost.

If we substitute the word 'teacher' for 'communicator' and 'class' for 'audience' much of it reads too close for continued comfort among either practitioners or observers of teaching. Some of this audience 'rejection' is particularly manifest in post-secondary education where the teacher has no immediate knowledge of how instructional sessions have proceeded (called 'feedback') in the form of disruptive behaviour that may occur in the face-to-face group. The feedback will be communicated in much more subtle ways such as the misunderstandings of processes or principles as revealed in student assignments, conversations with students outside, or sometimes inside, the group session and so on. I mention this only to emphasise the point that at these age levels, where class control or 'discipline' poses few problems, some ineffective communication or even 'non-communication' occurs. At the normal school age ranges, however, this lack of communication is sometimes hidden by discipline or control problems. Indeed teaching there is sometimes seen solely as a control process, and in certain circumstances this is a major achievement in itself, though it ought not to hide the fact that the basic concomitant of all teaching is learning.

LEARNING THEORIES IN TEACHING

It would be out of place here to discuss the nature of learning in any great detail, as parallel books in this series deal expertly with the topics (Leach and Raybould 1977; Riding 1977). Suffice it to say that broadly learning theories can be classified into either stimulus-response theories or cognitive theories, though there is much interchange of ideas within and between the two schools and much blurring of the boundaries between them. Perhaps the best known of the *stimulus-response theorists* follow the doctrines of Skinner (1953 and 1969) and stress the process of shaping the learner's behaviour through what is called *operant conditioning* — providing reinforcement when behaviour is close to that which the experimenter desires, and withholding reinforcement when it is not. (A teacher praising a pupil or ignoring a pupil would be crude illustrations of such behaviours in a practical situation.) There are other stimulus-response theorists following the Miller and Dollard (1941) line with its more complicated *drive–cue–response–reward* theory, and still others who, following Guthrie (1952), stress what is called the *principle of simple contiguity.* This theory states that stimuli accompanying a response tend on their reoccurence to evoke that response. (An example would be our reaction of feeling thirsty when we see a film of drinks being poured as in a TV advertisement — the stimulus of drink evoking thirst.)

The other school of thought as represented by the *cognitive theorists* has given rise to group participation processes, problem solving and highly permissive, unstructured environments for learning. Muscular responses are held to be less important than brain functioning. Insight rather than reward, understanding rather than practice, cognitive structures rather than habits are all emphasised by the cognitive theorists in looking at the instructional process. An interesting attempt to marry the two approaches has been that of Sheffield (1961) where he has tried to translate cognitive and organisational principles into stimulus-response theory and back again, as demonstrated by his analysis of the procedures involved in assembling the complex components of an aeroplane part.

In so far as we have taken any formal line on learning in this book we have inclined towards both a cognitive and a stimulus-response viewpoint. We concentrate on the latter (behaviourist) theory in this chapter particularly because social learning, a topic we shall deal with at some length, builds upon such a theory. However the work of Sheffield (1961) suggests a very positive way forward in integrating both viewpoints, as does the work of McLeish (1976) and his collaborators. We shall return to McLeish later. Certainly such evidence as is germane to this problem suggests that, first, the tutorial or didactic aspects constitute only a small part of learning — much of it taking place within or without the classroom unintentionally or accidentally, a process that psychologists term *incidental learning*. Second, knowledge of results or *feedback*, in fact knowing in some way whether you are successful, or proceeding correctly, is fairly crucial to learning. Third, that there is no clear link between research evidence and the 'best' methods of teaching. In the few cases where the same methods have been used across different areas of content and programming styles, most findings have not been consistent, other than the finding that able students or pupils do better (Maccoby and Markle 1973). While it is interesting to consider how teachers tend to vary their methods of teaching according to their own hunches, and in the light of the results obtained by their pupils, discarding methods that yield poor results and extending methods yielding good ones, it is also interesting to consider the context in which teaching takes place. (It would be nice to record, as a psychologist, that teachers use explicit psychological theories as a basis for their planning of teaching methods, but from long personal observation and experience I fear such usage is not the general rule. There may be some implicit or incidental usage of psychological theory but there appears to be little specific usage.)

TEACHERS' JUDGEMENTS OF NON-VERBAL BEHAVIOUR

The difficulty teachers have in utilising many of the cues emitted by pupils is illustrated by the studies of Maccoby, Jecker, Breitrose and Rose (1964). They sought to develop principles for teaching teachers how to 'read' the non-verbal behaviour of pupils. Standardised lessons were taught by the teachers and followed immediately by tests of pupils' comprehension. Later, close-up films of individual pupils were played back to the teachers who were asked to judge, on the basis of each pupil's gestures, facial impressions etc., whether or not the pupil understood what was being explained to him. The test data provided a criterion or standard against which the accuracy of each teacher's judgement could be compared. Training in the content analysis of such filmed episodes showed modest but statistically significant gains in teacher accuracy. The authors, however, after wide subsequent exploration, have not been able to identify the particular cues that formed the basis for the teachers' improved judgements. This suggests that, while some cues can be isolated and studied experimentally, the systematic use of such cues in the classroom as a basis for judging the success of interaction is as far away as ever it was.

TEACHERS' GOALS

The experiment of Maccoby and his colleagues suggests that the whole process of teacher–pupil communication needs a closer examination to establish the social context in which learning takes place. Closely interwoven with this learning context are the goals teachers have that influence their day-to-day tasks. Argyle (1972) in discussing teaching as a professional social skill posits one main and two subsidiary goals for teachers. The *main goal* is 'to increase the knowledge, understanding or skills of the pupils' or, in other words, to ensure that they learn something. The *subsidiary goals* are 'to increase the motivation and interests of pupils' and 'to maintain order and discipline'. The goals are subsidiary because the primary goal cannot be achieved without them. We did suggest earlier, however, that sometimes the teaching process remains at the subsidiary level, i.e. maintaining order and discipline, and there can be quite valid reasons for this.

The nature of communication

We have already stressed at some length the view that communication is transactional in nature. That is to say both teacher and pupil perceive the fact that they each partake of interactional sequences in greater or lesser measure, as shown by the amount of attention displayed, or dialogue engaged in, between them. Figure 4.1 shows the processes involved. The teacher is compelled, by his inner tensions, to *communicate* some information related to that tension and chooses a *transmitter* or *medium* for it. This medium is usually speech but it may be a gesture (such as banging a desk with a ruler) or, more rarely, physical contact such as a nudge or push. The information must be arranged or encoded in the form of a message which is appropriate to the circumstances, that is to say the teacher will need to use forms appropriate to the pupils — not a whisper if a pupil is reading a book nor a wave of the hand if the pupil is not looking. The message passes through what is called the

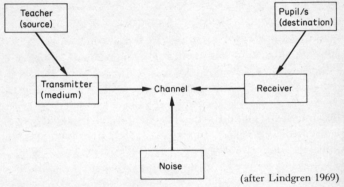

(after Lindgren 1969)

Figure 4.1 Diagrammatic representation of communication as a transaction

communication channel. This channel is not located anywhere other than in the sense organs and cognitive structures of the participants. So if the teacher speaks to the pupil the communication channel consists of the teacher's idea (cognitive structure) which is conveyed by his voice (transmitter/sense organ). The idea is heard (receiver/sense organ) by the pupil and decoded (cognitive structure) by him.

What communication specialists call *noise* can intervene at any point to obscure either communicator or audience and distort the message sent and received. *Noise* need not be actual or literal sound. It may well take various forms, such as the teacher using a level of language too advanced for the pupil to understand, or conversely, on the pupil's part, a too elementary or elemental explanation for the teacher to understand. Both cases can result in a 'shutting off' on the part of either and possibly create attitudes and hostile reactions that will make *noise*, that is, hinder communication as illustrated by the comment, 'What you are shouts so loud that I cannot hear what you say.' We shall look at this phenomenon of noise again later.

COMMUNICATION IN GROUPS

We have already discussed in detail the nature of groups and their interaction which all depend on the communication process for their existence. In looking at classrooms one advantage of splitting a class into subgroups lies in the reduction for the teacher of the number of potential channels of communication. For example, in a class of forty, if each child were to interact with every other child in the classroom, the number of interactional pairs could total 780 (as calculated by Thelen's (1960) formula $\frac{n(n-1)}{2}$ where n is the total number of group members). This calculation of course takes no account of the teacher interacting with anyone, which would raise the number of interactions to 820. By splitting the class into, say, five groups of eight pupils the number of interactional pairs for each group could be reduced to twenty-eight. The amount of *noise* is thus theoretically reduced because each pupil group member is linked to his peers by a noise-free channel that enables him to work without distraction. The use of groups then can be a powerful aid to the teacher in both learning, motivational and disciplinary areas. Because noise is reduced, communication becomes easier.

Linked to this easier communication is the nature of messages sent. Whenever a person is in the presence of another or others and communication occurs, the message sent contains both *explicit* and *implicit* information. The *explicit* information the teacher conveys might be 'You must look very carefully at this diagram to see the working parts of the engine' while the *implicit* information might be the mood of the teacher ('I love engines'), the status of the teacher ('Aren't I wonderful to know so much about engines?'), the role of the teacher ('They need to know about this and I must tell them') and so on.

When the teacher talks to groups as opposed to whole classes he has the opportunity of perhaps sitting with pupils and more chances of interacting with one pupil at a time. As we saw when we discussed *person perception* the spatial arrangement of teacher and pupils affects the type of interaction they engage in. Because physical distance between teacher and pupils is reduced in a small group, so psychological or social distance tends similarly to be reduced. As a consequence of this, supervision is tighter, pupils can fool about less and the teacher can adopt a less formal stance or, in technical terms, reduce the *status differential* between himself and the pupil. The more formal stance inevitably used when interacting with the whole class can make for another distracting influence in terms of *implicit* information. But at times, of course, it is necessary, valuable and effective, such as when a teacher is telling or reading a story, and the direct information conveyed may be less important than the overall attitudes engendered in the pupils. Such occasions generally gain from interaction with a wider audience. There is, too, the point that in sheer narrative episodes, whole class methods may be the best way of conveying information. Some enthusiastic, but I think misguided, practitioners at all levels of education feel that most teaching should be with small groups alone. It really depends on what the teacher is trying to do; in some cases small groups will be applicable, in other cases whole classes or even a number of classes. The selection of the appropriate groupings too will be one index of a teacher's professional skill, and training could play an important part in this.

THE IDENTITY OF THE COMMUNICATOR

The importance of the nature of implicit information is seen to greatest effect in an audience's attention to a communicator. A *high-status communicator* will generally be given greater attention than a *low-status* one, if indeed the latter gets any attention at all. The establishment of a communicator's identity is particularly important in the communication process, since it will determine audience reaction. In terms of the concepts we discussed at the beginning of the chapter, audiences are more likely to reduce the *noise* in the communication channel when attending to a high-status person. In the school situation, teachers are certainly regarded in terms of high and low status by pupils (and by colleagues) though, not surprisingly, there is little empirical evidence of this because it is a very sensitive area for investigation. Hargreaves (1967), in his very perceptive study of social relations in a secondary school, touches on it by implication but has had to omit, on grounds of confidentiality, much important information about the area. 'It might be advanced that pupils recognise two areas of status: the first being concerned with control and discipline, 'We don't fool about in Mr Smith's class — he makes it too tough', and the second with content and learning procedures, 'We learnt a lot about West Africa last year in Mrs Jones's class — she made it really come alive'. There may be (and often is) a relationship between those aspects but it is possible for one to exist without the others; namely for strong control to be exercised without any learning taking place, and for interesting learning to be taking place without any apparent control function being actively exercised. Where the content of lessons is interesting, learning procedures probably produce a built-in control function, since arousing pupils' interests leads to their following closely the subject matter and exercising appropriate behaviours (i.e. self-discipline) to that end.

MENTAL SET AND STATUS DIFFERENCES

The perceptions of any audience concerning a communicator give rise to the development of a kind of group or individual *mental set*, which means a favourable or unfavourable predetermined attitude to the message communicated. This attitude will be dependent on the *status* of the communicator and I should perhaps make it clear that I am using status in Hollander's (1964) sense as we discussed in chapter 3, not in any sense of moral or intellectual worth or standing but solely as *an index of the relative position of persons within a hierarchy arranged primarily on a reward basis.* So a high-status person in the sense used here would be likely to have a higher salary, a bigger office, more secretarial help etc., than a low-status person.

Therefore a high-status person may be perceived as uttering profundities which, uttered by a low-status person, would be dismissed as unexceptionable or even trivial. A low-status person may say something profound but, because the audience is tuned in to the status aspect, it may be perceived as very ordinary. High-status persons receive greater attention too, because their status makes them more visible. (We discussed visibility in chapter 3.) Probably in classroom interaction with pupils *visibility* is not the influential phenomenon it is between some teachers themselves and in the educational world at large. In the classroom the majority of teachers are exposed to their audiences for fairly equal amounts of time and there is not the psychological or social distance between teacher and taught that exists between educational administrator and teacher, for example.

Headteachers, however, represent a different level of status in which this 'visibility phenomenon' is generally more apparent than with class teachers, though their visibility is often greater than that of educational administrators. Nevertheless some headteachers do not stress or emphasise their visibility, preferring what is called minimum visibility or, in the jargon, a low profile. As one looks further up the status hierarchy both psychological and physical distance tend to increase and so does visibility. A number of educators have access to a lot of formal and informal channels of communication, including the media, and the status of such communicators tends to attract a following often based on quite false perceptions, but sufficient to ensure a high-status 'mental set' and predetermine attitudes. Low-status communicators too can sometimes become visible, though often for the wrong reasons, e.g. a teacher striking a child and getting his name in the newspapers following a court case. Visibility is clearly a mixed blessing, whether arising from a high or a low status, and not always the joy some observers think it is.

The nature of social learning

The place of the learning process has already been briefly discussed, in so far as it was necessary to outline the process as a concomitant of teaching. We ought, however, to look a little more closely at aspects of social learning as they relate to teaching. Such social learning will embrace not only facts but also attitudes and behaviour — in fact a good deal of incidental learning. It will therefore be closely connected to the teacher's subsidiary goals of increasing motivation and interests and of maintaining order and discipline.

The area of social learning was formalised in the works of Bandura and Walters (1963) and Bandura (1971), who emphasised the role of social variables to a greater extent than traditional-learning theorists. We will examine their theories from the teaching point of view, though it is important here again to stress that the influence any one teacher exerts on a child is likely to be limited. So when we speak of the teacher 'doing this' or 'teaching that' and the child responding in certain ways, the child's response is not necessarily an enduring change. If *learning* is the term that *psychology gives to relatively permanent changes in a person's behaviour that result from his experience*, then any one teacher will be lucky to be able to point, if he can point at all, to one or a few permanent changes in a pupil that can be attributed to his own teaching. The cumulative effect of several teachers over a period of time may be learning in a pupil, but pupil maturation (i.e. the pupil getting older) may equally be the cause. The teacher perhaps should not regard himself as the causal agent of pupil change but as the provider, at all times and within the limits set by the school environment, of the conditions wherein change may take place. As any teacher knows, many pupils perform an arithmetical operation, or remember a date, or write a sentence one day, and are quite incapable of the same behaviour the next. It is extremely hard to pinpoint the moment of learning at a single point in time, if in fact learning, as previously defined, occurs measurably at all. This makes the social context of learning (and hence of teaching, since teaching is the act of providing the environment where that learning is supervised, controlled, aided etc.) of great importance.

The first aspect to relate is the part *imitation* plays in the pupils' acquisition of new patterns of behaviour or in changing pupils' responses to different kinds of stimulus. Pupils imitate the behaviour of others they regard as significant to them. This phenomenon has been delineated in the term *significant others* first coined by Sullivan (1940) and elaborated in greater detail, for example, by Kuhn (1964). The others may often be teachers, but can be fellow pupils. Imitation provides a short cut for the learner to acquire social behaviours, because it eliminates much wasteful random behaviour. Such random behaviour would occur if we had to depend on his going through the often tedious process of trying out responses and seeing whether they were approved of by others (what is technically called 'reinforcement'), gradually dropping those that were not approved (or reinforced) and eventually acquiring the correct or appropriate behaviour. The acquisition of language might be quoted as one example of children imitating the speech of others, rather than their building up words and sentences by a system of the approval (or reinforcement) of one word at a time. (This view of course would represent a behaviourist one (e.g. Skinner 1957) vigorously rebutted by Chomsky (1959) and Miller (1965), for example. For a general description of children's acquisition of language see Brown (1977) in this series.)

IMITATIVE BEHAVIOURS

Obviously the place of reinforcement (or approval) is an important part of the social-learning process since the pupil learns to imitate behaviour that brings approval. Though he may imitate whole behaviours, such as speaking, his first imitation may be far from reproducing the original exactly, and reinforcement causes imitative behaviour to be persisted in over time. This reinforcement will of course apply to the learning of both cognitive behaviours (such as language) or affective behaviours (such as altruism).

Staub's experiment   A field experiment illustrating modelling behaviour in which sixty-four children of infant-school age participated is reported by Staub (1971). Each child interacted with the experimenter individually in playing games etc., the experimenter either adopting a warm, friendly approach (*nurturance* or reinforcement) or a non-committal one (*no*

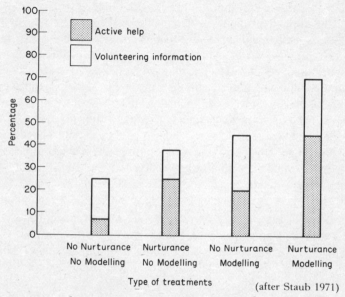

Figure 4.2 *Percentages of two types of response in four treatment groups*

nurturance or no reinforcement). She then left the children and went into an adjoining room, explaining to each child that she was doing so either to help a child there who was apparently distressed and crying (*the modelling condition*) or to check on a child there (*the no-modelling condition*). The children then heard sounds of severe crying and distress from the adjoining room which were in reality the recorded sounds of such a child and not a distressed child in person. Children exposed to the *modelling condition* showed 'active help' and 'volunteered information' at a statistically significant higher level than children exposed to the *no-modelling condition*. 'Active help' took the form of going into the adjoining room to see the child; 'volunteering information' consisted of saying, when the experimenter returned, 'that something had happened in the other room'. Similarly, children exposed to the *nurturance* condition were significantly higher in their level of 'active help' than children exposed to the *no-nurturance* condition.

The four treatments were equalised across the sixty-four children so that sixteen received *no-nurturance* and *no-modelling* exposure; sixteen *nurturance* but *no-modelling* exposure; sixteen *no-nurturance* but *modelling* exposure and sixteen *nurturance* and *modelling* exposure. Figure 4.2 sets out the pattern of responses by each of the four groups. The superiority of *modelling* and *nurturance* (reinforcement) combined over any of the other treatments is clearly shown but the social importance of *nurturance* (reinforcement) as a stimulus to 'active help', even in the absence of modelling, is clearly indicated in the second histogram.

Reinforcement   We have already referred to Skinner's theories of learning, in which reinforcement figures prominently as the central idea of his research dealing with instrumental or operant conditioning. He says of the way reinforcement itself affects learning:

> By arranging a reinforcing consequence, we increase the rate at which a response occurs: by eliminating the consequence we decrease the rate. These are the processes of operant conditioning and extinction. (Skinner 1963)

Stevenson and Hill's experiment   Such reinforcement could be a powerful weapon in a teacher's armoury, since I suspect appropriate modelling behaviours in the general life of the classroom, as illustrated by the Staub experiment, are not always so explicit as in the controlled situation reported there. A teacher cannot always provide a model from his own behaviour because of the circumstances of his control function and the distance between himself and his pupils, but reinforcement is readily to hand. Stevenson and Hill (1966) report an experiment where individual children were given a large number of marbles and were required to insert them into a box through one of two holes. The experimenter let each child proceed in inserting marbles for a while, noting which hole he used least. He then started saying 'good' when the child put a marble into the least-used hole, or, in technical terms, provided *systematic reinforcement of the desired behaviour.* The children's choice of the least-used hole gradually increased in frequency.

ATTENTION

Page's experiment   Obviously in interpersonal relations one of the most powerful reinforcers is *attention.* Getting the attention of another person is generally rewarding, while being ignored is generally unrewarding. In the teaching stiuation itself (as opposed to the purely experimental one) the importance of attention is illustrated by the work of Page (1958). He asked seventy-four randomly .chosen teachers in American high schools and junior high schools to divide pupils' objective-type examination papers they were currently marking into three groups. (Objective-type means a type of test where there is one agreed answer, for example, *man* is to *wife* as *knife* is to —: the correct answer being *fork.*) The *first group* received 'free comments' on their papers in which the teacher wrote whatever he thought relevant. The *second group* received standardised comments, e.g. all B-graded papers had the comment, 'Good work. Keep at it,' written on them. The *third group* had only the score and a letter grade inserted on the papers. When the pupils were next examined pupils who had received the first 'free comment' (*maximum attention*) scored at a statistically signifi-cant higher level than on their first occasion. Pupils in the second group with standardised comments (*some attention*) showed some gain in scores but not as high as in the first group. The third group of pupils (*no attention*) who had only the score and grade on their papers showed no gain whatever.

Page asked the seventy-four teachers before the experiment how they thought their comments would affect their pupils' performances. The general view seemed to be that the pupils with higher scores and grades would do better but weaker pupils would be likely to act in an opposite manner to any suggested by the teacher. The results showed, however, that pupils receiving the most attention, i.e. all those with free comments, whether A- or F-graded students, showed measurable improvement. It seems that attention has direct reward value and amounts of attention directly affect behaviour, the behaviour in this case being the ability to score on objective-type examination tests.

In Skinnerian terms the free comments were perceived by the pupils as a *reinforcing consequence of better behaviour* and they were thus encouraged to increase its frequency. This has important implications for teacher control, since people generally act in accordance with how they perceive others think of them. In this experiment some 'weaker' pupils ('weaker' being those with inferior initial test scores) nevertheless perceived themselves to be better as the result of the maximum attention they received from the teacher. Hence they made a measurable improvement. While it might be objected that it is somewhat dishonest to encourage 'weak' pupils to believe themselves to be better than they are, it is perhaps important to stress that a teacher is charged with getting the best from his pupils and hence he often needs to avoid presenting facts as they actually appear to be. (Doctors may similarly hide the 'true' nature of a serious illness so as not to make the patient's mental attitude worse than it already is.) A pupil publicly labelled 'weak' will more than likely act up to this description, a pupil labelled 'hopeful' will more than likely prove to be so. Literal truth in human relations in general, and in teacher–pupil relations in particular, often serves no-one's interests, least of all the pupil's. A nineteenth-century divine enunciated a perfect conditioning principle about social behaviour when he said 'that we should always behave toward our enemy as though he would one day be our friend'.

Just as attention can be shown to facilitate learning, so withdrawal of attention can have the opposite effect and retard learning. This phenomenon is known as *extinction*. In other words the teacher/experimenter ceases to reinforce the pupils/subjects and the level of performance slowly begins to fall — eventually returning to its former level. In the classroom, too, the influence of other pupils is also a powerful one in a reinforcing sense and we shall return to this topic again later.

What the teacher will be aiming at, in terms of the pupil's behaviour, will essentially be the attainment a *pupil's own self-control*, rather than the imposition of *continuous teacher control*. Such self-control will aid both of a pupil's own social development and the smooth operation of the learning process in general. We have constantly referred to the situation where behaviours occur as the result of teacher stimulation and reinforcement, but cease when the teacher withdraws — perhaps being extinguished altogether after a short period. The opposite behaviours to these, which all teachers are likely to want to encourage, are such as to guide the child largely to regulate his own behaviour without the imposition of external pressures. Such a process is of course a gradual one, the development of which is difficult to chart — like all behaviour that is usual or normative. Where a child fails publicly in the attempt to regulate his own behaviour and deviates noticeably from the usual or normative state (termed deviant behaviour) this, by its very definition, gets itself noticed and recorded much more quickly.

BANDURA AND KUPER'S EXPERIMENT

Obviously the procedures of imitation, reinforcement and modelling all have critical parts to play in pupils' self-controlling behaviour. Modelling is a particularly important ingredient in the self-controlling process. As Bandura and Walters (1963) say:

The influence of models in transmitting patterns of self-rewards and self-punishments has received attention in only one experimental study [Bandura and Kupers 1964]. Children participated in a bowling game with an adult or a peer model, the scores, which could range from five to thirty being controlled by the experimenter. At the outset of the game, the children and their models were given access to a plentiful supply of candy, from which they could help themselves as they wished. Under one experimental condition the model set a high standard for self-reinforcement; on trials in which the model obtained or exceeded a score of twenty, he rewarded himself with candy and made self-approving statements, while on trials in which he failed to meet the adopted standards he took no candy and berated himself. In the other experimental condition, the model exhibited a similar pattern of self-reward and self-disapproval, except that he adopted the standard of ten, a relatively low level of performance. After exposure to their respective models, the children played a series of games on the bowling apparatus in the absence of the models. During these trials the children received a wide range of scores, and the performances for which they rewarded themselves with candy and self-approval were recorded.

It was found that the children's patterns of self-reinforcement closely matched those of the model to which they had been exposed; moreover, they tended to reproduce the self-approval and self-critical comments of their model. Thus, although both groups had access to a plentiful supply of desired material reinforcers, the children who had adopted a high criterion for self-reinforcement through imitation utilised these resources sparingly and only when they achieved relatively high levels of performance, while children who were exposed to the low-standard model rewarded themselves generously even for minimal performance.

THE TEACHER AS MODELLING AGENT
In other words the modelling agent, the teacher in this case, needs to be certain that his own behaviour is beyond reproach if the modelling is to be effective. While remembering that their

influence, in the amounts of time spent with pupils as compared with parents, is not the largest (though I suspect much more influential in some cases than the actual 'time spent' would suggest), it is difficult to escape the conclusion that teachers are not always as conscious of their modelling effects on pupils as they might be.

For example, it is not unknown for some teachers to appear in TV news films (films that are often concerned with some kind of school dispute or other) in dress and hairstyles that by any standard would be judged to be untidy. Now both the central issue (the dispute) and the image (untidy appearance) are not the norms of conformist behaviour. Hence by the public at large, and by pupils in some cases, the teachers are seen to be 'violating prohibitions' and judged accordingly. I am not here judging the moral quality of their behaviour, only pointing out the likely consequences of their actions. The modelling behaviour they provide will influence pupils' behaviour well beyond the area of where the modelling incident itself took place. In the context of our present society, where roles are achieved rather than ascribed or 'given', the teacher has both more chances of achieving a distinctive positive model (because no inhibitory rules are laid down) and of failing to achieve it (because no guidelines are given). Obviously his own personality characteristics will often be the determinant of the modelling behaviour he provides.

THE WORK OF McLEISH AND HIS COLLABORATORS

Finally, to draw together the threads of a number of points we have made in this section on social learning, the important work of McLeish (1976) and his collaborators (McLeish, Matheson and Park 1973) is particularly relevant. We mentioned earlier the process of language acquisition as being a controversial field where Chomsky (1959), for example, had attacked the behaviourist views of Skinner (1957). McLeish suggests that Chomsky's criticisms of Skinner are in reality a criticism of psychological research itself, which research, Chomsky suggests, reveals only trivial aspects of behaviour. Chomsky essentially posits mental states as explaining behaviour, states, that is, which cannot be verified experimentally, as opposed to the Skinnerian concepts of explaining behaviour, namely the processes of stimulus, response, reinforcement and shaping which can. McLeish, by the use of the most sophisticated observational and computer techniques, analysed the group behaviour of each participant in a student group, second by second, with a view to seeing whether such Skinnerian concepts were enough to account for the changes of their behaviour as they went about their learning task. In fact Skinner's concepts were completely vindicated and found to be quite adequate to explain the adaptive behaviour of the participants in acts of communication. As McLeish (1976) says: 'The implications of this finding for psychology and education are manifold. Communication is a complex human skill which we have shown to be under the control of contingencies of reinforcement.' He then continues by saying that though many of Skinner's basic theories come from studies of animal behaviour, and we need to devise a more complex and dynamic model taking account of the *social* environment and the *human* subject, such

. . . basic principles of explanation require no supplementation when we pass from motor and secretory behaviour to the specifically human symbolic ('verbal') communicative behaviour. No mentalistic constructs or other hypothetical variables are needed to clarify the nature of human activity in a social situation — indeed, they merely confuse the basic simplicity of the scientific explanation.

These are strong words indeed, and not all professional workers will agree with them, but McLeish's findings are very important in stressing that even quite complex human behaviours may be experimentally verifiable in terms of such stimulus-response theories. In this chapter we have largely used such theories to describe and demonstrate the social nature of the interaction process. In the work as a whole, however, we have strayed, quite deliberately, from the path of exclusivity, believing that to describe the social context needs social and socio-psychological theories as well as purely psychological ones.

Reference groups

We referred earlier to the importance of the influence on a pupil of other pupils, both for the modelling process itself and as a reinforcer of social behaviour. Other pupils constitute what Sherif (1963) termed a *reference group*. That is a group 'to which an individual relates himself or aspires to relate himself as a part psychologically.' Now a pupil will have various models to which he may wish to relate himself in addition to the model of his own peers. One set of such models will be authority figures like teachers and parents; another will be figures from the entertainment and sporting world. The latter group and his own peer group are likely to be more appealing to him than authority figures because they are younger, apparently more 'interesting' and certainly more visible. (I put 'interesting' in inverted commas only because these models appear to be doing interesting and lively things. This is their public image. In actual fact few jobs are more boring in some ways than a pop star's, as individuals and groups at the end of their careers, e.g. the Beatles, will frankly admit). But a pupil's attitudes and behaviour will often be modelled on what he imagines to be the attitudes and behaviour of his reference group. A reference group, then, may be one to which the pupil actually belongs, as in the case of the school class itself, or alternatively one to which he accredits himself, e.g. as a follower of a pop group. It is important to note too that a reference group may in fact be an individual as well as a group of persons. Certainly such reference groups will be an important influence on the individual pupil's 'social reality'. That is, many of his general ideas about life, what he esteems to be true, essential and worth believing in, will be what the reference group themselves openly or hiddenly express or are felt to express.

THE COMPARISON FUNCTION

In speaking of reference groups in a normative way, that is, in the way that such groups set and enforce standards of conduct and belief, the *comparison function* ought not to be forgotten. Pupils, especially in the older age ranges, are regularly engaged, in greater or lesser degree, in establishing the reference group as a standard or comparison point against which they may compare themselves and others. The teacher, aware of these processes in the pupil, can often find that his task in the control sense is not as difficult as it might appear, because the *comparison function*, which all pupils engage in to some degree at some time, causes such pupils' own self-perceptions to be fairly ambivalent. That is to say, to perceive oneself as a conformist is often felt to be as threatening as to perceive oneself as a rebel. The pupils' natural reference group, then, is likely to share somewhat different aims and values from those their teachers hold. However, on the other hand, pupils will not always want to be seen to be, or perceive themselves to be, at variance with the values of their teachers. Hence conformity and rebellion will coexist in most pupils in different degrees at different times. Many pupils, perhaps after some inner struggles, will want to believe that they conform because this is the correct and proper thing to do. They will not want to believe they conform from the fear of being thought different, because this type of conformity suggests weakness and dependence. Teachers too, in their relations with senior colleagues, will show many of the same characteristics concerning conformity.

Tuddenham and McBride's experiment   An interesting experiment by Tuddenham and McBride (1959) illustrates how many persons attempt to achieve a balance between the threats posed by conformity and deviance. The investigators analysed the responses (on questionnaires and in the form of unstructured answers to questions) of students who had yielded appreciably to the pressures of group colleagues in a modification of Asch's experiment (see chapter 1). Many of the responses to the questions showed that these 'yielding' subjects nevertheless regarded themselves as independently minded. A detailed examination of the responses showed that such individuals selectively perceive that while they may have moved towards the group norm they have not moved completely over to it. Hence because of their *selective perceptions*, i.e. perceiving what they want to perceive, they can satisfy both their belief in independence and their belief in conformity. The way such conflicts are resolved has some similarity to the phenomenon of cognitive dissonance (Festinger 1957) to which we shall return.

Pupils' views of reference groups   Given the importance of other pupils — the peer group — and their influence on a pupil's behaviour, his need to identify with them may cause him, in public, to support their judgements or imitate their behaviour while privately rejecting them. The importance of reference groups lies in their potential to influence an individual's behaviour. This potential is there even when an individual wrongly perceives what the reference group's opinions actually are, or rightly perceives the reference group's actual view, while believing it to be wrong to follow it. Pupils are not necessarily acting on direct instructions from, or from direct knowledge of, their reference group when accused of deliberately making a disruptive act, though sometimes very young children will say 'John told me to drop the book', thus implicating John and revealing in their innocence the person they are taking as their reference group. Sometimes older children too (often, in my experience, those who are somewhat unimaginative) revert to this type of explanation, genuinely believing that they have been 'instructed' to act thus. As a rule, however, pupils tend to support what they believe to be the opinions held by the majority of the pupils, or by the most powerful pupils, or by the pupils whom they most desire to be like. When the class group in general is working together well and is finding much satisfaction in its communal activities, there will be less discrepancy between what pupils say in private and what they say in public. A class group that is fulfilling and satisfying to an individual pupil often tends to produce actual changes in his beliefs and in his outward behaviour. Sometimes, of course, the reference group produces behavioural conformity by means of the threat of punishment. The individual pupil may fear ostracism from, and non-acceptance by, the group so much that he conforms, even though the threat is chiefly in his own mind and does not explicitly arise from the reference group.

Teachers' views of reference groups   Such observations perhaps give a clue as to how teachers need to be apprised of the importance of the reference group as an influence on classroom behaviour. When they first take charge of classes, say at the beginning of the academic year in September, reference groups may not be much to the fore in the pupil's mind, since during the long summer vacation each pupil has been continuously engaged in another milieu outside the school. The influences of his own peer group and of authority figures will be weak and only the third group that we described (entertainment and sporting personalities) may be anywhere near influential, and even they may be relatively dormant as far as public appearances go. Hence the teacher has the opportunity to provide positive learning experiences and to develop group cohesion so that reference groups — at least as far as those that arise in the school are concerned — will be broadly in line with his own policy and intentions. Or, as we indicated in the previous paragraph, from the pupils finding much satisfaction there will be less discrepancy between their public and private statements. Obviously, reference groups other than fellow pupils will not lie dormant indefinitely but can be used positively. In understanding a pupil's social learning the teacher needs to attempt to determine what reference groups the pupil is using, what importance he attaches to each of them and what he is learning from them. Perhaps some of the most psychologically significant acquisitions from reference groups will be particular attitudes and values that influence behaviour both within and without the classroom. What needs to be stressed is that every year a teacher has a chance to make a fresh start and certainly influence in some degree, by his own planning behaviours, the type of reference group that emerges within the classroom, which in turn will exert a powerful influence on the kind of learning that takes place within the classroom itself.

Cooperation and competition

Reference groups, and the peer group in particular, will play some part in the way pupils coalesce together in adopting a cooperative or a competitive stance towards the learning tasks in hand. But the teacher also has a crucial part to play in arranging how both *competition* or *cooperation* are emphasised and how they emerge in the type of organisation and activity that finally occurs in the classroom.

COLEMAN'S EXPERIMENT

A good illustration of how the school's *group norms* influence *peer group behaviour* is provided by Coleman (1961) in his comparison of two boys' schools. In the school where the peer-group emphasis was on competition he found that intelligence-test scores of boys with the highest grades A or A— for school work were well above the average scores for the school as a whole. In the school where there was no emphasis on competition the As and A—s were only just above the school's average on intelligence-test scores. There seems no reason to suppose that the teachers in the first school valued grade attainment any more than those in the second. The implications were clearly that the peer group's influence was either strongly in favour of attainment or gave no particular emphasis to it. Coleman argues that, as far as the boys were concerned, organised athletics provided the only corporate outlet for the pupils' positive competitive energies and left only the individual outlets of negative competition in terms of grade attainment. He argued for a shift from competition between pupils (*interpersonal competition*) to competition between groups (*intergroup competition*), so that the different structure of rewards in the latter case would lead to more harmonious pupil development.

GOLDBERG AND MACCOBY'S EXPERIMENT

Goldberg and Maccoby (1965) elaborated the classic work of Mintz (1951) in terms of an experiment with infant-age children. In Mintz's experimental situation individual subjects had to pull a number of paper cones out of a single narrow-necked jar. When the subject was put under pressure, by the likelihood of receiving a reward on the basis of how quickly he could remove all the cones from the jar, 'traffic jams' developed at the neck of the jar because of a subject's anxiety to get all the cones out in time. When, however, groups of participants, as opposed to individuals, received a single score on the basis of the total time taken to remove all the cones from the jar, they worked out an efficient strategy, among themselves, of taking turns so that all the cones were withdrawn smoothly in a relatively short time.

In Goldberg and Maccoby's experiment two groups of infant-age children were involved, thirty-two boys and thirty-two girls, and they were divided into four groups of sixteen, each of one sex. One group of sixteen boys performed a cooperative task, in subgroups of four, eight times (each time is technically called a 'trial'), but before every third trial the subgroups were changed. The other group of sixteen boys performed the cooperative task also in subgroups of four, but consecutively for the eight trials. The two groups of sixteen girls were similarly split into the *changing* condition and the *no-change* condition. After the eight trials each of the four groups of sixteen were split into new subgroups of four and performed another eight trials consecutively. Essentially the experimenters were comparing the performance of the *experienced* cooperating children, the ones who had four changes of group formation and working, with the *inexperienced* cooperating children, the ones who worked consecutively for the first eight trials, all together.

The cooperative task selected for the experiment was building a tower with wooden blocks within a fifteen-second period. Each child in the subgroups of four had eight different coloured blocks so that his/her own contribution to the subgroup's effort could be measured. After receiving instructions to the effect that individual efforts would be rewarded, and that each child should work as quickly as possible, the children were given fifteen seconds on each trial to build their towers. Each child's score could range from 0 to 8 blocks placed on each trial. There was no credit for blocks placed after the signal to stop. Further, towers that collapsed between the stop signal and before the experimenter could count their number were treated as if they fell during the trial. The results of the first eight sessions, when experimental conditions differed in both groups, are shown in the following table:

Average number of blocks placed per trial by *changing* groups	45·4	32 children on 8 trials
Average number of blocks placed per trial by sub-groups of above	5·7	4 children on 8 trials
Average number of blocks placed per trial by *constant* groups	72·0	32 children on 8 trials
Average number of blocks placed per trial by sub-groups of above	9·0	4 children on 8 trials

The differences between the two groups are statistically significant. In discussing their experiment the authors suggest, in the light of their analysis of children's behaviour during the first eight trials, that when experimental conditions were not common certain children in the *changing* groups had time and opportunity to exercise coercive dominance, while others virtually withdrew from the situation by placing few or no blocks in each tower. They suggest that it takes time to develop genuinely cooperative processes, because the group needs first to devise means of controlling any individual children inclined to be dominant. Such control was sometimes shown in the experiment by the other children knocking down the tower built by the dominant children. That cooperative behaviours are learnt is illustrated by the fact that at the sixteenth trial (that is after eight continuous trials in stable conditions) both groups' performance were gradually approaching a common standard, the *changing* groups having placed seventy blocks over trials nine to sixteen, the *constant* groups having placed eighty-three over the same period. Perhaps over a further eight trials their standard might well have been almost indistinguishable.

COOPERATION AND COMPETITION AMONG PUPILS AND TEACHERS

This behaviour discussed here is of course behaviour in a problem-solving group whose members are of equal status. Perhaps the lesson to be drawn from it is that cooperation to achieve a corporate end can be learnt under appropriate circumstances, and competition extinguished, by both the pressures of external events and the pressures exerted internally within the group. Much of our general social life, as was said earlier, proceeds on a cooperative basis because *role behaviours* so prescribe that it should. For example, when I write out a cheque for cash in my favour and take it to my bank I receive the amount of money written on it from the bank-clerk. Our role behaviours of client and clerk lay down what is to be performed. In this situation, as in the experimental one just described, the participants, client and clerk/work groups of children, are of equal power and status. However, when considering teachers and children the differing status and power positions call for the teacher, in the final analysis, to order, demand or request compliance, and the role of the children calls for them to obey.

In any situation where there is an authority figure and a subordinate, while the former may talk about 'achieving, getting or obtaining cooperation' he may in fact mean obedience and compliance. Though obviously teachers do not, as a rule, exercise their power so markedly, and realise that some of the most effective procedures for learning are democratic ones, there is, as was said earlier, an element of underlying compulsion arising from the teacher's role — even when cooperative learning environments are the norm. In such cooperative situations competition for the teacher's attention can lead to pupils engaging in competitive behaviours so as to be noticed and to present themselves more favourably. Competition can be minimised, at least as far as its harmful effects are concerned, but not eliminated. Indeed a recognition of the fact that both types of behaviour coexist in all of us would considerably reduce some of the apparent conflict between what educators say and what they in fact do.

We discussed earlier how 'productivity' was difficult to define as an educational outcome, though easily defined as an industrial outcome, such as by the number of motor cars produced in a given month. The ambiguity, then, of the educational situation leaves vast room for competition in all forms, and not least between teachers as well as between pupils. A teacher can even use his cooperative teaching methods as an index of how 'good' or 'effective' he is, that is, in a competitive way. This is in my view quite justifiable, but it shows how competitive educators can be, indeed may have to be, in seeking recognition, given the absence of tangible productivity figures like those available in industry.

Punishment and control

The question of punishment, either as an internal or external control influence, is obviously pertinent to the whole process of social learning. If we associate *positive reinforcement* with reward, then with punishment the associations should logically lie with *negative reinforcement*. However, this is not in fact the case. As Wheldall (1975) says:

> Negative reinforcement sounds like punishment but the two are by no means the same. Negative reinforcement has the effect of increasing responses by the termination of an aversive stimulus whereas punishment consists of presenting the aversive stimulus in an attempt to reduce the frequency of responses. Skinner considers punishment to be a rather

unreliable and time-consuming way of preventing responses from occurring and does not give it much emphasis in his writings. In passing, we should note that removing positive reinforcers is also a form of punishment.

This gives a clue as to why teachers' direct punishment techniques such as using negative reinforcers (verbal reproofs — 'Stop talking', 'You have done this appallingly' — or, notwithstanding the strictures on teachers using physical contact, striking or shaking a pupil) do not work as effectively as myth has it. As was said, negative reinforcement can often increase (bad) responses rather than extinguish them. Perhaps we should concentrate on the removal of positive reinforcers, as Wheldall suggests, as one key to effective classroom control which by its 'depriving action' will influence the behaviour of pupils.

As we said, punishment has a *retribution* element and a *control* element. The *retribution* element arises from the view that misdemeanours unbalance the natural order of justice in society and must be 'paid for' by the transgressor enduring punishment. The *control* element stems from the view that, unless misdemeanours are checked, society will not be able to function smoothly. We might call these the 'moral' and the 'control' elements. Now the classroom is 'society in miniature' and teachers share in the confusion that abounds at large. I suggest that many of them, quite rightly, see punishment only in terms of a control function without the thought, in their capacity as teachers, of any wider dimension attaching to it. The general public, however (particularly those in the older age brackets), and perhaps parents too, whose views sometimes impinge on teachers directly, are vaguely conscious of the wider view, though they lack any clear idea as to how the retribution functions and the control functions are to be distributed. Musgrove and Taylor's (1969) investigation, for example, showed something of the disparity between the views of teachers and parents on both moral and social aspects. Teachers greatly underestimated the importance parents attached to moral training (moral element) and overestimated the importance parents attached to the teacher as an agent of social advancement (control element).

MADSEN, BECKER AND THOMAS'S EXPERIMENT

An experimental illustration of how positive social reinforcers (smiles, praise, contact, nearness, attention), or their absence (what Wheldall calls 'removing positive reinforcers'), influence the classroom behaviour of pupils is provided in the work of Madsen, Becker and Thomas (1968). Two classes of children, one at the infant-age level and one at the junior-age level, were chosen. In the first, two children with a high frequency of problem behaviour were studied. In the second, two children were initially selected but one dropped out after the experimental procedure had begun. (It is to the credit of the experimenters that they show the difficulties of real-life field experimentation by not abandoning the experiment, even though their sample was cut effectively by 25 per cent.) The actual pattern of the children's problem behaviour was established by observation and called the 'baseline'. The two teachers concerned then underwent an intensive workshop course on behavioural principles, which provided them with a rationale for the experimental procedures they were to introduce in their classes. These procedures were introduced one at a time and the effect on the three pupils (called the 'target children') observed by trained recorders. The teachers' behaviours were also rated, although at less frequent intervals than the children's.

The children in each class were subjected to a schedule of teacher behaviours which consisted of various combinations of the following (sometimes applied one after the other, sometimes two or more conditions applied simultaneously):

1 *Baseline conditions.* The teacher conducts classes in her own typical way.

2 *Rules.* The teacher states short rules for children to follow (e.g. 'Sit quietly while working').

3 *Ignoring inappropriate behaviour.* The teacher ignores any child's behaviour which interferes with learning or teaching

(unless one child is actually physically attacked by another). Not surprisingly the teacher found this the most difficult of the procedures to follow, but its importance in the experimental design can best be illustrated by the actual instructions given to the teachers:

> The reason for this phase of the experiment is to test the possibility that attention to Inappropriate Behaviour may serve to strengthen the very behaviour that the attention is intended to diminish. Inappropriate behaviour may be strengthened by paying attention to it even though you may think that you are punishing the behaviour.

4 *Praising appropriate behaviour.* The teacher praises a pupil's achievement, positive social behaviour, following group rules (e.g. 'You're doing fine', 'That's a very good job'), the general rule being that praise and attention was given to behaviours assisting learning.

The following table shows the results obtained, in respect of one of the problem pupils studied, which are illustrative of the main findings of the study.

Behaviour category	% intervals in which inappropriate behaviours occurred		
	Highest	*Lowest*	*Increase*(+) or decrease (−) *at end of observation period*
	Beginning of Observations	*End of Observations*	
Baseline	over 80%	40%	−
Rules	over 40%	over 80%	+
Ignoring	100%	over 80%	−
Rules and Ignoring and Praising	40%	over 20%	−

In summary, the main findings showed that Rules alone had little effect in reducing inappropriate behaviours (the figures in the table under Rules do in fact conceal that there was a temporary drop before the big climb); Ignoring Behaviour needs further classification (again, the above figures conceal a drop to 40 per cent before rising again to 80 per cent); the combination of Ignoring and Praising resulted in the greatest drop in inappropriate behaviours. In the latter connection, when a comparison on *inappropriate behaviours occurring* was made between (1) conditions where praise was emphasised and (2) conditions where it was not, the lowest number of inappropriate behaviours occurred in 'praise' conditions. Further, the differences between the two conditions were statistically significant.

Practical implications We have dealt with this experiment at some length because it is a very good illustration of the

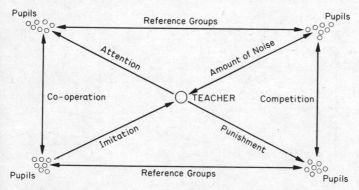

Figure 4.3 Diagram of teacher interaction with class (traditional view)

procedures involved in dispensing and withholding reinforcement, in education, according to strict schedules and under carefully controlled conditions. The original paper also enlarges on the effects on teacher and pupil behaviours and makes the point that these systematic behaviours can be taught to teachers (though I suspect doing so would need a lot of public-relations groundwork both here and in other Western-type cultures). It further notes that, although the study was formally concerned with only a few 'target children', the beneficial effects on the children in both classes were noticed by teachers and observers alike. This phenomenon, where children, other than those to whom a teacher's remarks are addressed, note and act upon the remark or the implications of it, is called *the ripple effect* (Kounin and Gump 1958). The teacher's behaviour can be likened to a stone thrown into a pond. The stone sends out ripples that affect a much wider area than the immediate point where the stone hit the water. Finally the authors note that 'unless teachers are effective in getting children "ready to learn" their technical teaching skills are likely to be wasted'. This has been our theme throughout this book.

THE TEACHER'S POSITION
Much of the literature on teaching naturally stresses the view that the teacher is at the heart of it. Indeed he may be. Figure 4.3

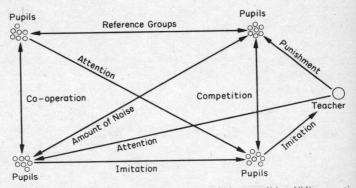

Figure 4.4 Diagram of teacher interaction with class (non-traditional/idiosyncratic view)

would represent the stance we have taken in this chapter in the mainstream tradition. However, it is only fair to point out that from the pupils' point of view the teacher himself may be seen as fairly superfluous at times to their main concerns as represented in figure 4.4. This puts the teacher outside the social and even learning concerns of the pupil, and here the teacher is seen as only remotely impinging on classroom activities. In reality I suspect that teachers, as seen by individual pupils or groups of pupils, move from their position in figure 4.3 to their position in figure 4.4 and back again several times a day. All the social phenomena we have discussed can apply to pupils as well as to teachers. So pupils too have different statuses, provide different models for imitation, act as reinforcers, give or withhold attention and communicate with differing amounts of noise. Pupils can act in these ways either singly or in groups or, more rarely, as a whole class.

So the teacher's primary task of increasing the knowledge, understanding and skills of the pupils depends on both his effectiveness in increasing pupils' motivation and interests and in maintaining order. But even if he is effective in the latter task, a pupil's intellectual growth will in some measure depend on circumstances outside the teacher's control — the pupil's innate abilities and dispositions, his home and cultural background, the parental support he enjoys and so on. What we have explored here are some psychological bases for the interaction that takes place in the classroom, in the pursuit of the teacher's primary and subsidiary goals.

5

Teacher behaviour in organisational settings

The organisational setting

Though we have so far discussed the nature of teaching primarily in so far as it concerns the teacher and his pupils in the classroom, we need to realise that teachers and pupils are parts of larger groupings, namely schools, that exert great pressures upon their senior members, the teachers, to act in certain ways and to achieve certain goals. So headteachers, as official leaders of the whole group, or heads of departments, as official leaders of parts of the whole group, can say that the school will assemble at a certain time, that subject X or Y will be taught, that certain examinations, internal or external, will take place and so on. These days such direction will tend to be fairly mild, and will usually be preceded by the head consulting his senior colleagues, so that the direction has the nature of making public what has already been agreed in private. Nevertheless, among the worries class teachers have, interaction with 'bad' heads or heads of department are likely to figure prominently — often to a much greater extent than interaction with 'bad' pupils. The relation between schools and heads, as between all organisations and leaders, is a reciprocal one: heads develop schools and schools develop heads. As we have seen in discussing leadership, when people come together to form groups for a purpose, they are likely to find or create the leadership they require. The result of interaction between leadership and the creation of a group for a purpose is an *organisation.*

THE NATURE OF ORGANISATIONS

Katz and Kahn (1966) note that organisations are social devices for accomplishing some stated purpose efficiently through group means. They see organisations as open systems — a concept psychologists have borrowed from biology. Any organisational system can be considered as an energy system that has *inputs, transformation processes* and *outputs*, technically called the *input–output model*. Hence in a school the *input* would be pupils, teaching materials, books and money for various purposes (e.g. outside visits for pupils). The *transformation process* would take the form of teacher talk/pupil discussion in whole classes or groups, pupil assignments, homework, informal interaction between pupils, discussion and so on. The *output* would be educated individuals.

Another view of the nature of organisations is the *bureaucratic model* where individuals within a system occupy a number of roles dependent on each other's and termed *interlocking roles*, reinforced by what Weber (1947) calls 'rational legal authority'. Applying this model to the school, we see that teachers are expected to teach, but their willingness to do so is ineffective unless pupils are willing to learn. So the teaching and learning roles are mutually dependent on one another or *interlocking*. To ensure that the transformation processes occur smoothly and in an ordered way, organisations develop rules and regulations to which are tied penalties and rewards. It is, perhaps, important to mention that the term 'bureaucracy' is used here neutrally, to describe the administrative aspects of an organisation. In popular usage 'bureaucracy' is synonymous with the rigid enforcement of detailed rules and regulations, by members of an organisation, with sinister overtones of control and compulsion. Certainly some bureaucracies have such characteristics but our concern is not with them. All formal organisations (even down to the one- or two-teacher village school) have at least a minimum of bureaucracy, as we have defined it.

SCHOOLS AS ORGANISATIONS

The reason for looking fairly closely at the organisational field is to provide an introduction to the study of schools which in the modern Western world are the first type of organisation people encounter in their lives. Currently, too, many secondary schools are often bigger organisational units than the shops, offices or factories in which a large number of their pupils will eventually be employed after leaving them. This transition from looking at teaching in small units of behaviour to looking at it in large, global terms is best justified in the words of Kahn, Wolfe, Quinn, Snoek and Rosenthal (1964) who say 'Organisations are reducible to human acts: yet they are lawful and in part understandable only at the level of collective behaviour.' This comment was made before my own wider plea for placing psychology in a social context (Cortis 1973) if it is to have relevance, though my motivation arose from similar dissatisfactions. The attempt of the social and industrial psychologists of the fifties and sixties to explain the behaviour of small industrial work groups, and such phenomena as job satisfaction and job performance, was not wholly successful precisely because it ignored the organisational setting in which it occurred. Not surprisingly, psychologists were led to conclude that the study of the organisation itself would give a more complete picture. Prominent among such workers were the social psychologists at the University of Michigan such as Katz and Kahn (1966) and Likert (1967).

Bidwell (1965) in a review of theory and research on schools as formal organisations notes the conflict between two major tasks of the school: *first*, to coordinate the activities of individual teachers and schools in order to ensure minimum uniformity of outcomes and, *second*, to maintain sufficient latitude *vis-à-vis* the public and the employing authorities to allow teachers and heads to exercise professional judgement. The earlier description of the 'input–output' model does suggest that a school is like a factory with production lines devoted to producing a range of identical children all with common characteristics. The implication of Bidwell's comments seem to be that the task, while an input–output one, is to attempt to produce individuals as different from each other as possible or, in his own words, to ensure 'minimum uniformity of outcomes'. The influence of the public in Britain and the employing authorities on schools has not as yet become anything like the force it is in the United States, though Bidwell's words are a warning of what may happen here in time. Both parental influence and the influence of employing authorities are increasing, and seem likely to do so even further, especially in periods where economic values — 'Is it worth the cost?' — are paramount.

ORGANISATIONAL CATEGORIES

Schools are technically termed *maintenance organisations* (Katz and Kahn 1966). That is to say, they are engaged in the socialisation of people and maintain their numbers by performing the functions of education, indoctrination and training. Other maintenance organisations include health and welfare agencies such as hospitals and old people's homes. The organisational category, then, in which schools are placed — *maintenance organisations* — can be compared with the other three categories of organisations: *productive, adaptive* and *political.*

Productive organisations (sometimes called *economic organisations*) manufacture goods and provide services such as food, shelter and clothing. *Adaptive organisations* create knowledge, develop and test theories and apply information to existing problems. A university would be an example of such an organisation. *Political organisations* are concerned primarily with maintaining the social structure, that is, with global rather than with individual concerns. The state is the prime example — mobilising society against threats from within and without, and providing a framework of law to allow the exercise of individual and group rights and responsibilities. Within this definition would come various subsystems of government, political parties, trade unions and so on.

PSYCHOLOGICAL MOTIVES FOR WORKING IN ORGANISATIONS

The motives for working in organisations in general, and

teaching in particular, are inevitably mixed, and are likely to entail rewards other than monetary ones. Of particular importance perhaps is the satisfaction of an individual's psychological needs. Though persons become involved in the work of organisations for a variety of reasons, not least economic ones, the need to find both identity and affiliation with others ranks high in their order of priorities when considering entry to, and staying in, a job. An early theory in the literature as to the nature of people's motives was advanced by Maslow (1943) in which he lists five goals to which men's behaviour is directed, as follows:

1 *Physiological needs* (such as food, water and drink) which are basic to the survival of the organism.

2 *Safety needs*, that is the need for a threat-free environment.

3 *Social needs*, including the need to be accepted by others, for affectionate relations with others, to be part of a group.

4 *Esteem needs*, such as self-respect.

5 *Self-actualisation needs*, that is the importance of self-fulfilment, the need to do things that fulfil a person's potential.

Perhaps particularly important in this list, number 5, the 'need to self-actualise' is worth commenting on because it draws attention to the fact that people do certain activities for no reason beyond such a need. We accept that people play games, listen to music or read novels for no other reason than that they are valuable activities in their own right. Perhaps people work in large part for the same reason.

Maslow further suggests that these needs are arranged in a hierarchical order, and a person works his way through them, only passing on to the higher ones (4 and 5) when lower-order ones have been satisfied. This is a good example of a theory that is attractive but is as much an article of faith as anything else because it cannot be easily tested. Psychologists sometimes favour it because it seems to embody the important general postulation that *behaviour is initiated to rectify imbalance in physiological functioning* (Wolf 1970). It is useful because it points to the fact that many motives may direct behaviour and that people may engage in activities because of other extrinsic motives.

Herzberg's two-factor theory (Herzberg 1966) is a theory having some parallels to Maslow's because it points out that people like doing things they find valuable, but unlike Maslow's it has generated some research. Herzberg and his colleagues (Herzberg, Mausner and Snyderman 1959) found that, on questioning people about their work, the same people seemed to be describing different activities when they said they were satisfied from when they said they were dissatisfied. This was puzzling. Normally it might have been expected that the presence or absence of a certain condition (say achievement) would give rise to satisfaction or dissatisfaction. The investigators examined in detail the way in which people described their jobs. Their findings suggested that good times at work were the product of factors like achievement, advancement, recognition, responsibility and the work itself. Bad times at work were the product of factors like poor company policy, interpersonal relations, salary, security and poor working conditions. Herzberg (1966) in commenting on these findings suggests that man is motivated by two basic and yet different needs — the *need to avoid pain* and the *need to self-actualise*. He notes:

> The human animal has two categories of needs. One stems from his animal disposition. It is centred on the avoidance of loss of life, hunger, pain, sexual deprivation and other primary drives, in addition to the infinite varieties of learned fears that become attached to these basic drives. The other segment of man's nature . . . is man's compelling urge to realise his own potentiality by continuous psychological growth. Perhaps there are primitive glimmerings of [this] characteristic in sub-human species. Recent experiments on the curiosity and manipulative drives of animals suggest such possibilities.

If he is right, then improved salaries, improved interpersonal relations and so on will serve only the need to avoid pain and will not necessarily benefit the organisation's aims directly. What will be of benefit will be to serve the need to self-actualise by giving organisational members more recognition, responsibility and the like. Like many relatively simple ideas which have an immediate superficial appeal but appear less attractive under critical scrutiny the reception has been mixed, and King (1970), for instance, has pointed out examples of studies that suggest people at work do in fact feel bad about factors like achievement, responsibility etc., just as they feel good about them.

SUBJECTIVITY OF SOCIAL AND PSYCHOLOGICAL PHENOMENA

The controversy is a good example of the way social phenomena are likely to be fairly subjective. If beauty is in the eye of the beholder, then so is truth likely to be, because each (beauty and truth) cannot be measured objectively like phenomena in the physical sciences. Here the problem is that studies which support Herzberg's theory have invariably used his technique of inquiry, while those studies which do not support it have used other techniques. Vroom (1964) explains these discrepancies in part by noting that the stories people tell of their work vary according to whether people are describing times they perceive as good and fulfilling, or times they perceive as bad and frustrating. In 'the good times' they say how well they themselves did, while in 'the bad times' they often become defensive and tend to put the blame for their unhappiness on others. Wall, Stephenson and Skidmore (1971) have noted that subjects under pressure to show themselves in a good light (such as at an interview for a job) produce data that tend to support the existence of the two-factor theory, whereas the data of subjects not exposed to such pressure do not tend to support the theory.

We are here of course, in considering Herzberg's and Maslow's theories, thrown back on to the nature of what the word *need* means because it is a word consistently used (and misused) in psychology. Psychologists use the word as a technical term to refer to *a condition or state that can be measured independently of the behaviour the organism initiates to change such a state.* In animal studies, for example (from which a number of simple learning theories concerning human behaviour have been derived), we infer that because the animal has suffered a weight loss after being deprived of food his *need* is for food. However the word *need* also has currency in everyday language to denote the importance of things to people. So we can say 'he needed the coat' and 'need' here refers to the individual's motive for wanting it; it does not refer to any condition that is identified independently from behaviour.

Herzberg in fact uses the word 'need' in its everyday sense, and while apparently true of the particular groups of subjects he studied, such 'needs' are not necessarily experienced by everyone working in organisations irrespective of their individual psychological state. The same strictures also apply to Maslow's outline of needs. In many ways both theories are attractive ones but the evidence for them is fairly equivocal in empirical terms. People work for a variety of reasons or needs, apart from the sheer economic necessity of maintaining themselves. Their motivations are fairly mixed. Characteristically professional/technical workers and managers are said to be more satisfied with their work than clerical/unskilled workers — the former mentioning more often *ego satisfactions* such as personal involvement, self-expression and so on, the latter mentioning *extrinsic satisfactions* like pay and conditions (Gurin, Veroff and Feld 1960).

Teachers, however, constitute an 'in-between' group whose satisfactions are likely to be a mixture of both *ego* and *extrinsic* elements. This mixture arises because of the nature of the job and the uncertain status accorded to it. While certain of both Maslow's and Herzberg's 'need' theories would seem to apply to the teaching act, the parallels are not really exact ones (although the *esteem*, *self-actualisation* and *pain avoidance* needs in particular come to mind) because teaching is different in nature from other white-collar or professional occupations, such as those in hospitals and in social work. The organisational context is different and hence needs are different also. We shall return to the topic of the nature of teaching as compared with other kinds of professional work later on.

THE INFORMAL ORGANISATIONAL STRUCTURE IN SCHOOLS

Along with the *formal structure* of the organisation that we discussed earlier, and parallel to it, is the organisation's *informal structure*. This is formed by the social relations that develop among members and is an important line of communication among and between them. For example, though in hierarchical organisations like schools, communications are supposed to move from the headteacher downwards via perhaps deputy head, head of department and finally class teacher and pupil, it sometimes happens that the class teacher knows what is coming before the head or 'intermediate' staff do. The informal lines of communication, or the 'grapevine', have done the job before the formal lines can be activated. In this connection the role of secretarial or administrative staff is important, since they are often the recipients of information incidentally, through handling telephone calls and the like, which they can sometimes by accident, or on purpose, communicate to junior staff, thereby short-circuiting official channels. If we look back to our earlier discussion we see that persons at the centre of informational networks achieve a high degree of power by virtue of their handling of information and by their disseminating or withholding it. Though such persons may not be of high status in informal terms, their informal status may be high.

Similarly, the *informal structure* extends to role performance, and sometimes behaviour, so that what is said to happen and what exactly does happen are often dissimilar and even at times contradictory. For example, syllabuses may specify material for teaching that is in fact never taught to certain groups of pupils because it is regarded as too difficult for them, but its retention avoids awkward questions being raised by school inspectors. Or senior members of staff may state how busy they are to an outside visitor (or sometimes to a staff member) but seem always to be out of the school on courses, conferences or even at professional men's or women's luncheon clubs. If tackled about the latter they might well say that their position in the community at large demanded their presence at such a function.

They could well be right too, for much valuable work of a professional nature can be accomplished at such apparently 'recreational' affairs.

Goffman (1968) summarises the position neatly when he says 'This contradiction, between what the institution does and what its officials must say it does, forms the basic context of the staff's daily activity.' The discrepancy between formal and informal behaviours — or when people propose one course of action publicly and then privately follow another, perhaps even opposite, course of action — gives conspiratorial overtones to human behaviour, particularly in organisations, since as we have said, public and private goals are not so easily reconciled there. The problem in meeting such ideas in an educational context is that teaching is traditionally supposed to be an activity with a moral dimension to it so that we talk of the 'good' teacher but seldom of the 'good' lawyer (Wilson 1962). Hence ideas about organisational life current enough in other spheres of work are looked upon with some fear when it comes to the teaching situation. The atmospheric overtones in teaching are still in many ways those of 'playing the game' of delicate personal contacts between teacher and pupil and of mystique and veneration. To suggest that motivations are more mixed and that teachers even tell lies about themselves and their duties seems, in some quarters still unacceptable.

The management function in schools

At the beginning of the chapter we spoke about headteachers as the 'official' leaders of the organisations we call schools and it seems appropriate that we should now deal, in a little more depth, with the *management function*. Yet class teachers are also holders of managerial jobs in part, and what we have to say will, in some degree, be applicable to them also, for such management theories can be applied to the way in which a class is managed as well as to how a school is run. There is, however, a somewhat critical difference which I think resides in the concept of *psychological distance* we dealt with earlier. The difference is this. When the teacher interacts with his class, psychological distance protects him in some degree from any pupil's unfavourable reaction striking home and wounding his (the teacher's) ego. So he can dismiss a pupil's grumbles about himself (the teacher) by the psychological mechanism of *rationalisation* which, briefly described, is the response pattern by which we explain away situations in which we find ourselves, in such a way as to justify our actions. The teacher might say, for example, 'Johnny Jones is always like that — grumbles about everything' and psychological distance generally ensures that the pupil doesn't answer back. When, on the other hand, the teacher interacts with senior colleagues, such as the head, he may still engage in the same behaviour. The psychological distance is, however, reduced (and especially today in the informal atmosphere among many current school staffs). Hence not only may the head answer the teacher back but other colleagues might do so as well in support of the head. So I would say that the management of pupils and the management of teachers are both similar and yet different types of behaviour. Hargreaves (1972) discusses the matter of head–staff relations with his customary lucidity:

Of major interest to the social psychologist is the effect of the autocracy on the relations between the head and the staff. With respect to the teachers the principal effect of the autocracy resides in their dependence on the head. They are dependent on the head in three main areas. First, they are dependent on him for internal promotion, since the distribution of the additional monetary allowances is at the head's discretion. These allowances can make a substantial difference to a teacher's income and are thus regarded as important. Second, teachers have to rely on the head for a reference where a change of school or an external promotion is sought. Unless the head provides at least a satisfactory reference, a candidate for a new post is unlikely to find himself on the short-list. Since such references are highly confidential, a teacher may find it difficult to discover how good a reference he has been given. Third, the teacher depends on the head for various favours. Some of these favours can be of great significance. Recently, for instance, many Local Education Authorities have decided to leave the distribution of money to different departments within the school to the head's discretion. There are many other favours, great and small, at the head's disposal and by withholding them the head can make life difficult and unpleasant for a teacher. In these three ways it will pay the teacher to keep in the head's 'good books'.

As Hargreaves goes on to note, the result is that the teacher replicates the principal phenomenon of teacher–pupil relations so that 'pleasing teacher' becomes 'pleasing headteacher'. The way the teacher operates such a process might be summarised under the following three headings:

1 Find out both what pleases and displeases your headteacher.

2 Bring to his attention those things that please him and conceal from him those things that displease him.

3 Remember it is a competitive situation. The teacher must try to please his headteacher and yet avoid displeasing him more than do the other teachers in the school.

PROBLEMS OF MANAGERIAL AUTHORITY

Hargreaves's comments clarify my earlier point about organisational functions. In some ways management techniques have common elements. This applies whether the management is of children by teachers, or of teachers by heads, or, conversely, whether the management is of teachers by children or of heads by teachers. These two latter examples are not intended to be facetious, as Lowin and Craig's experiment (quoted in chapter 3) demonstrated. Management is a two-way process, though one in which we have customarily assumed the manager is formally and officially paramount. As we said earlier, however, teaching is in many ways basically a battlefield and, though the leader 'can't win them all', he will need to win the majority of his battles. If the management of teachers by heads, and of pupils by teachers, have common elements, one of them is the element of winning. Waller (1965) said of teacher–pupil relations: 'The teacher nearly always wins. In fact he must win, or he cannot remain a teacher.' The same is true of heads. They too must win or cease being heads, even in today's 'participatory' or 'consultative' climate. By this I mean that, in all spheres of work, including teaching, the move in recent years has been towards an informal pattern or 'climate' of behaviour where the bosses often consult the workers and together they jointly devise, agree and implement the decisions that are made in regard to work practices. The climate has not, however, altered the basic parameters or rules of the game, for as Hargreaves notes 'a change of image is not necessarily associated with a shift in power.'

Some teachers, however, still see the head as exercising a fairly despotic role whatever noises any head may make about 'the democratic approach'. Such teachers can experience an acute personal conflict if faced themselves with the prospect of promotion to a headship. Having perhaps themselves believed in an 'open' approach, they realise they may now be forced into committing exactly the same 'deceptions' they till now had accused others of doing. They are placed in the quandary posed by the following propositions:

1 *I hold the view that all managers/headteachers are manipulators/despots/authoritarians.*

2 *I am now a manager/headteacher.*

This is not the place to discuss the theory of cognitive dissonance (Festinger 1957) which the above propositions represent in detail and which is dealt with in a parallel book in this series (Fontana 1977), but the example serves to emphasise the importance of such a theory in the organisational context.

Certainly, as a former 'educational manager' myself, and from my own personal observations of people in such a situation, it seems to me that when such people were promoted their outward behaviour appeared to alter considerably towards the autocratic 'direction', though they still insisted in conversation that they were 'democrats'. This reinforces my earlier observations that managerial roles in education, as elsewhere, involve apparently contradictory actions on the part of the role incumbents and a good deal of apparent hypocrisy. It is a service to no one to pretend otherwise and I think that no guilt can be ascribed to people who behave thus, for such behaviour is not wicked but functional and inevitable.

DECISIONS AND ASSUMPTIONS ABOUT PEOPLE

In general, organisations have not focused on the creative human potential within themselves but have been very concerned with their bureaucratic functions, and this can be the case even with organisations such as schools that are supposedly devoted to the output of creative individuals. In fact some conflict often occurs between senior 'administrative' staff and lower-ranking staff members in the school in the area of decision making. The area of conflict is essentially whether their decisions are, or can be interpreted as, *educational decisions* or *administrative decisions.* For example, a typical problem might be the allocation of sixty children to three teachers for a teaching period in, say, language work. An administrative solution, especially if there are three classrooms available, might be the simple division of sixty children among three teachers into three classes of twenty. An educational solution might be that we need to look at the pupils' attainments/abilities and then take the forty of highest ability for some general exploratory-type lessons with one teacher. The remaining twenty will be divided between the other two teachers, that is ten apiece, for some remedial reading/activities. Obviously many such issues are much more complex than this but the example will serve to illustrate the essence of the problem.

McGregor (1960 and 1966) has conceptualised the task of management in terms of two theories he calls Theory X and Theory Y. Theory X is the conventional view of management: direct, prescribe, coerce, and check one's subordinates. Theory Y is McGregor's own, which attempts to integrate both the individual's and the organisation's goals. Here the manager leads, trusts, encourages his subordinates, allowing them the maximum freedom to plan their own destiny compatible with the organisation's goals. This theory is based on Maslow's work that we have already discussed which conceives man's primary need as being one of self-actualisation. Figure 5.1 contrasts the two theories which are, I think, important, not only to our understanding of administrative behaviour, but also to all organisational activities, since they describe an individual's assumptions about people generally. In this *person perception* sense, management in the school situation is a common activity whether it is concerned with heads and their teachers or with

THEORY X		THEORY Y	
Assumptions about People	Relevant Administrative Policies	Assumptions about People	Relevant Administrative Policies
1 Naturally inert, lazy, avoids work	1 Drive, 'motivate,' coerce	1 Naturally active, enterprising	1 Lead
2 Dependent	2 Direct	2 Independent	2 Use self-direction
3 Set in ways	3 Routine procedures	3 Growing	3 Open to change
4 Irresponsible	4 Check up	4 Responsible	4 Trust
5 Resistant, hostile	5 Fight, on guard	5 With you	5 Cooperation
6 Unimaginative	6 Prescribe	6 Creative	6 Encourage
7 Short-sighted	7 Plan for them	7 Capable of broad vision, long view	7 Plan with them

(after Watson 1966)

Figure 5.1 McGregor's two theories of management contrasted

teachers and their pupils. Such assumptions will obviously, in part, arise from the nature of an individual's personality whether, for example, he is extraverted or introverted. A parallel book in this series deals with the specific topic of personality (Fontana 1977).

ORGANISATIONAL CHANGE IN SCHOOLS

Carlson (1965) calls the American public schools (corresponding to British state schools) *domesticated organisations.* The school is in some ways protected and cared for like a domesticated animal — its needs guaranteed by its keeper. It has not itself to recruit its clientele nor struggle for survival, and its financial backing is not tied to the quality of its performance because of the reasons we have seen. From such consequences flow both the restricted need for, and interest in, change (since organisational survival is not dependent on performance levels) and the lack of interest in developing measures of efficiency. There is little competition on the basis of relative efficiency levels (relative, that is, to rival organisations) and hence little incentive to look critically at what school is doing. The law demands that children between certain ages receive education in school. While children exist so will the schools. The law is unlikely to be changed because it has the support of public opinion.

One of the obstacles to any form of change in all forms of organisational life is the fact that we are all enmeshed in the peer group or reference group to which we belong, and its survival is of great concern to each one of us, its members. The consequent difficulty of any proposed organisational change is that not only do the lines of communication and the processes (procedural, technical and organisational) present difficulties, but the participants themselves are in many cases at the least reluctant to change their mental viewpoints, if not downright hostile towards change, or perhaps even incapable of it. Let us look a little more closely at what the current position is concerning incentives and rewards in the school, though, under the influence of changing economic forces, some of the following conditions can easily apply to other forms of organisational life.

Status and normative rewards   In teaching, *status* assumes great importance though, as with *status considerations* in work generally, not a great deal is known about it. Argyle (1974) notes the relation of *status* to *job satisfaction*, independent of relative pay levels — though he is comparing teachers and manual workers. No doubt the former group would, for example, rather earn less for teaching than more for bricklaying, though to my own knowledge there is much disgruntlement over the relative pay levels of, say, heads and class teachers. Since in general monetary rewards cannot, at least for the foreseeable future, be tied to pupil learning, status itself becomes an important distributor of reward gratification in two ways. First, as a source of satisfaction and power in itself and, second, as a source of increased income to the teacher achieving a higher status.

Next we look at *normative rewards* which come from the manipulation and allocation of symbolic rewards within an organisation. (Examples would be a leader appealing to a member's 'sense of loyalty' or publicly esteeming his professional skill.) The person who infringes, or departs from, the normative pattern can feel uncomfortable and isolated. The classic studies of Sherif (1936) and Asch (1956), we have already noted, were experimental demonstrations of how norms developed in small groups and how group consensus has an effect that carries over to behaviour outside the context of the group.

In the school, as elsewhere, the *normative rewards* are often in competition with *peer-group norms.* Peer-group loyalty can also become a powerful and anti-organisational incentive as the school tries to put individuals in academic competition with one another and fails to direct *normative loyalties* towards *organisational goals.*

Hargreaves (1972) discusses the *mediocrity norm* among both staff and pupils. Though many pupils work harder than they publicly admit, most pupil groups have a *mediocrity norm* which is designed to conceal from the teacher how hard pupils are actually working. The motive for this is to ensure that the teacher does not apply these 'private' higher standards of work 'publicly and generally' to the whole pupil group. Teachers too, he says, have a *mediocrity norm* which similarly prohibits too great an enthusiasm or keenness. This shows itself in the staff's expectation that teachers will not arrive too early at school, or publicly work too hard such as in marking books at break-times, or be keen to undertake extra duties outside normal school hours. So *normative rewards* are by no means always positive and oriented towards the organisation's goals (one goal in practically all cases being that everyone in the organisation works as hard as he possibly can). *Normative rewards* can sometimes conflict with *status rewards.* Such a case would be where a teacher desired promotion (*status reward*) but to get himself noticed by his seniors had to show keenness in the areas we have described and thus incur disapproval from the staff (*normative punishment*). The same kind of dilemma faces the pupil who seeks publicly to work hard to achieve success.

Norms and the training process   Argyle (1974) talks about the practices in industry where *norms* are used both to *achieve an organisation's goals* (e.g. high output) and to *circumvent them* (e.g. in setting the limits of time wasting, scrounging, cheating on incentives etc.). He makes the important point that:

> People who have received professional training — e.g. doctors, scientists or accountants — usually internalise certain standards of conduct, which are sustained in isolation from other members of the profession, often in the face of considerable social pressures. Conforming to such norms helps the individual to sustain his professional identity and contributes to the long-term position of his profession.

This reinforces earlier comments about the nature of teaching. It is in reality neither an autonomous profession nor a truly bureaucratised occupation. Though teachers have received professional training there appears little in that training (or in the subsequent employment) that enables them to internalise certain standards of conduct and protect themselves and their position in society. Certainly they have some professional freedom of action and do not have to follow rules like 'pure' bureaucrats do, but the norms are not centralised in a professional institution such as, for example, the Chartered Institute of Accountants. Though he may receive some guidance from his trade union in professional matters, if he is a member of one, the teacher himself has basically to construct the norms to which he is to conform. While valid for him, they may not be the norms of his colleague in the next classroom, nor of the senior staff of the school, and a good deal of friction can arise with pupils who perceive Mr Smith as following one set of norms which are not the same as those of Mr Jones. Wilson (1962) discusses admirably a number of related issues to the topic of teacher professionalisation comparing teachers with other professional groups — particularly with doctors and lawyers.

Organisational climate in schools

We have now dealt at some length with various aspects of organisational life but perhaps the most significant is that which we term the *climate of the organisation*. This affects every aspect of an organisation's functioning. Taguiri (in Taguiri and Litwin 1968) defines climate as:

> . . . the relatively enduring quality of the internal environment of an organisation that (a) is experienced by its members, (b) influences their behaviour, and (c) can be described in terms of the values of a particular set of characteristics (or attributes) of the organisation.

In practice climate is measured principally by asking people to describe how they perceive their organisational environment, namely by asking members to reply to various set questions about aspects of their organisation in a number of ways; for example, how true such statements are perceived to be, or how characteristic of the leadership displayed they appear to be in the case of the particular organisation being studied. Taguiri distinguishes between the *subjective* and *objective* use of the term *climate*. The method we have described illuminates the *subjective* sense of the term, that is, as the members themselves perceive the organisation. The *objective* sense of the term would be the use of measures that were not ambiguous, such as the number and type of levels of authority in an organisation, or the number of formal rules it publishes. In general there are more examples in the research literature of the first type, the subjective, than of the second, the objective.

Though climate may be defined in the way it has been here, any of us connected with education, and I suspect quite a few of us without such experience, would soon 'feel' or 'gauge' or 'apprehend' the climate of various types of school if we were to visit a comprehensive school in an inner-city area and then visit one in an affluent suburb. In the first, not only would the buildings be more likely to be old, but the relations between staff and pupils would probably be characterised by an atmosphere of toughness. The pupils' approach to teachers would tend to be fairly formal and disciplinary problems would be in the forefront of teachers' minds — whether they were coping with them 'successfully' ('I bashed them hard the first day and then there was no more trouble') or manifestly failing ('I don't know how to cope with Form 4C — they're always cheeky and mucking about'). Hargreaves (1967) describes such a type of school and its ambiance very clearly. There would too, in general, be less stress on pupils' attainment and much more stress on keeping them in order. In the second case, the suburban school, not only would the buildings be likely to be newer, but the relations between staff and pupils would tend to be more informal and there would probably be a relaxed air about the place. Learning and attainment problems would be likely to figure in teachers' minds more than disciplinary problems; the evidence of this would be independent study in libraries and so on and less class-based and supervised work.

Now for illustrative purposes I have obviously generalised and we are all likely to know both of inner-city schools where, by first-class community work, the head and staff have created happy learning communities, and of suburban schools where, for a variety of reasons, a 'blackboard jungle' exists. Notwithstanding this I think my general summary is accurate and points out the difference between the different *climates*. Not only is it likely that such schools would be differentiated on climate in the *subjective* sense, that is, as members themselves perceive the organisation (school) in the form of different patterns of questionnaire responses, but it would certainly be possible to construct an *objective* measure that differentiated the respective climates. A measure of the latter kind, for example, would be the number of windows broken over a particular period of time in each school expressed as a percentage of the total number of windows in each school.

Classroom climate Each school, then, has its own climate, which is made up of a whole range of staff and pupil attitudes, expectations, values and personalities in combination. Each class will also have its own climate which will generally be in line with that obtaining throughout the school, though it would be possible to conceive of some differences between them, stemming basically from the role relations involved. For example, in the relatively tough climate of an inner-city school it would be possible to experience a more easy-going climate within the confines of, say, a class of slow-learning children where both the nature of the teaching–learning task and the typically gentler approach to such difficulties are specific to teachers specialising in this area of education. Flanders (1967) defines classroom climate in the following way:

> The words *classroom climate* refer to the generalised attitudes toward the teacher and the class that the pupils share in common in spite of individual differences. The development of these attitudes is an outgrowth of classroom interaction. As a result of participating in classroom activities, pupils soon develop shared expectations about how the teacher will act, what kind of person he is, and how they like their class. These expectations colour all aspects of classroom behaviour, creating a social atmosphere or climate that appears to be fairly stable, once established. Thus the word *climate* is merely a shorthand reference to those qualities that consistently predominate in most teacher–pupil contacts and contacts between pupils in the presence or absence of the teacher.

RESEARCH ISSUES

In research terms the concept of climate has been dealt with in a rather uneven fashion. The concepts of sociometry (Moreno 1953), and the work of Lewin, Lippitt and White (1939) in demonstrating the different climates associated with 'democratic', 'authoritarian' and 'laissez-faire' leadership, have already been discussed; these were both important illustrations of some of the factors involved. Withall (1951) developed a 'climate index' that involved the classification of teachers' verbal behaviour into seven categories which were further divisible into 'learner-supportive or -centred' and 'teacher-supportive or -centred' statements. A class was categorised as 'teacher-centred' when the statements were directive, repressive, disapproving, disparaging or defensive. A class was said to be 'learner-centred' when the statements were clarifying or reassuring.

Connor's experiment   Connor (1960) looked at eighteen classes of primary pupils in an urban area (681 children in all) and examined both the influence of the school and the interaction of the class group to determine the effect of each on climate. He measured climate both in terms of external tests, e.g. an 'Adjustment to School' questionnaire, and in terms of the actual sociometric structure of classes, as indicated by the pupils, together with observations of teacher–pupil rapport. Classes with 'good' climates, as measured by the tests, had children who interacted more freely and in a more friendly manner than the classes with 'poor' climates. The children in classes with 'good' climates showed more interest and enjoyment in their work and were more relaxed and less fearful than children in the classes with 'poor' climates. In other words, 'good' behaviours were associated with 'good' climates and vice versa. Connor, too, noted that, in his judgement, the type of climate produced is not so much dependent on the physical environment of the school (buildings, district, etc.) but upon what transpires within each class.

Harvey, Prather, White and Hoffmeister's experiment   Harvey, Prather, White and Hoffmeister (1968) examined the behaviour of 118 classes with an average of twenty-six pupils per class at the infant age level in an attempt to show the different classroom atmospheres engendered by two types of teacher, differentiated on the basis of their having either concrete or abstract belief systems. 'Abstract' teachers correspond to Withall's 'learner-centred' behaviour type; 'concrete' teachers to Withall's 'teacher-centred' behaviour type. The measures used were (1) ratings of the teacher's belief and concepts derived from experimental tests and (2) ratings of the 118 classes as a whole on thirty-one items of classroom behaviour (e.g. 'aggression toward classmates', 'adherence to teacher's rules'). In general the teacher's belief systems were shown to affect their classroom behaviours and these behaviours were significantly related to pupils' behaviours. For example, the pupils of 'abstract' teachers had a statistically significant level of higher involvement with classroom activities, were more active and showed higher levels of achievement. However, the difficulties of drawing firm conclusions from such research are shown by the authors saying:

> Theoretically, the teacher's behavior could determine the children's behavior, the reverse could be true, both could be determined by a third factor, such as the organisational climate, or the effects could be produced by the interaction among all of these factors. The possibility that the relationship between teachers' and students' behavior is a result of organisational climate is minimised by the fact that the concrete and abstract teachers, while selected from the same organisational climates, nevertheless differed markedly in their classroom behaviors, as did their students.

I mention these comments only to show the very real difficulties of research in this area and how even experienced workers can leave gaps. The statement about concrete and abstract teachers being 'selected from the same organisational climates' begs several questions. How do we know they were selected from the same climates? Were tests of climate (such as Withall's) given to check this? Were not climates part of the subject of the research? How, then, can we presume a condition as established (similar climates), which condition, in part, we are engaged in investigating? In investigating a problem we do not presume to know the answer, or part of the answer, before we begin. There could well be perfectly satisfactory answers to all of these questions but they illustrate the difficulty of disentangling the essence of what climate is and of demonstrating its independence of other factors.

RECENT WORK AND THE PROBLEM OF GOAL ACHIEVEMENT

Finlayson (1975) in a succinct review of recent work has described his own elaboration of the subjective questionnaire of Halpin and Croft (1973). The elaboration consisted of seeking teachers' perceptions of their school climates in three extended areas, as well as pupils' perceptions of their teachers and of each other. The three extended areas were concerned with (1) the headteacher's administrative and decision-making behaviour, (2) the behaviour of heads of departments, and (3) the nature of communication between the school and the community. Particularly interesting are the behavioural factors derived for pupils, teachers, heads of department and headteachers. Basically the items in all areas split into *task* and *social* considerations, along the classic lines of group behavioural theory. Finlayson does not dodge either the issue of the complex nature of perceptions and their validity, that is, the degree to which they measure what they say they are measuring (in this case climate). He makes the most important point that, in school settings anyway, we have not *tested* any theories of organisational climate against goal achievement.

As we noted in chapter 1, the hallmark of any body of knowledge calling itself a science is traditionally that any theory it proposes is a testable theory, no matter whether the test proves true or false. Perhaps the fact that many of the theories arising from an educational context are by no means testable explains the ambivalent status of education as an area of study, though it seems to me that it is a situation we have to live with in the real world. That is to say, while it would be possible to set up experiments to test many of the theories and concepts we have discussed, in some cases it would be necessary to distort the experimental conditions so much that no valid conclusions about real life could be drawn from such experiments.

As we have previously indicated, the goals of schools are ambiguous — hence our use of analogous situations from other forms of organisational life where a main goal can be identified (e.g. making a product) and conclusions can be drawn in terms of a measure outside the 'climate', like productivity. The topic of climate is a good illustration of our difficulty in verifying a concept by use of experiment in the field where psychology meets education. All of us know (from our experience as pupils in our own schooldays if nothing else) that schools differ markedly in atmosphere or climate, but it is hard to say how or why those climates differ from each other, and even harder to say how the very notion of climate itself is perceived by us.

Mayo and the Hawthorne experiment

The classic illustration of the effects of climate is provided by the experiments carried out by Elton Mayo fifty years ago, the implications of which are as yet neither fully understood nor worked out. They exemplify the maxim that 'great things cannot have escaped observation' — a statement which, though true of the social sciences, as of other disciplines, perhaps needs the qualification that 'observation' needs continual redefinition. In the social sciences many of the basic observations have probably been made and it is primarily in our definition and redefinition of them that progress lies. Mayo's Hawthorne experiment is an example of that redefinition of which we spoke — the basic experiment yielding more and more insights as time goes by. Mayo was an industrial psychologist who began his career in Australia at the turn of the century, concerned then, as we are now seventy years later, with a way of reconciling the worker's need for belongingness with the conflicting allegiances of the complex world in which he finds himself. (For 'worker' we could substitute 'teacher/pupil' or any other kind of organisational member, excepting the freelance artist/writer, and even the latter can be drawn at times into the organisational net.)

THE EXPERIMENT

In 1927, now nearly fifty years ago, Mayo began what seemed likely to be a very modest experiment at the Hawthorne, Illinois, plant of the Western Electric Company. (Strangely he has never himself made a full account of it, the best one probably being in Roethlisberger and Dickson (1964).) For some years the company had been concerned about the need to produce more telephones, or in technical terms 'the need to raise the level of productivity', against a background of worker complaint. In the beginning various efficiency experts were called in and prescribed the usual panaceas — changing rest periods, stepping up the lighting intensities in the workrooms, altering work hours and so on. The results, however, were inconclusive.

Mayo and his co-workers began by isolating two workrooms, one a 'control' group, where conditions would be left the same, and the other where the illumination would be noticeably increased. Output of telephones increased measurably in the 'highly illuminated' room but so did it in the 'control' room too. The team of investigators, led by Mayo, were puzzled. The next stage involved isolating a group of six women operatives from the others and over five years introducing a whole series of changes in rotation. The changes sampled various incentives, for example *economic incentives*, such as piece work (piece work means literally 'paid by the piece' and in this case meant the more telephones assembled, the more money earned), *fatigue-reduction incentives*, such as more rest periods, *economic and hunger-reduction incentives*, such as a free hot meal, and *avoidance-of-pain incentives*, such as shorter hours. An important factor was the presence of an observer who sat with the girls listening to their problems, telling them about the experiment and asking for advice and information. Finally the girls returned to the original conditions existing before the experiment began: no piece work, no rest pauses, no shorter hours and no free meal. Output was the highest ever recorded.

IMPLICATIONS FOR TEACHERS

So there it was. The experimenters realised that higher productivity lay in the attention paid to the whole workforce engaged in the experiments, whether subject to the particular experimental conditions or not. The subjects had been made to feel important, to feel special, to feel they counted within the organisation, not as mere cogs within a machine, but as a congenial group. However, with the passage of time there have, not surprisingly, been critics of the research. Prominent among them is Carey (1967) whose principal criticism, from a replication of the study, was that material reward was the chief influence on work morale and behaviour, rather than any other incentive.

Notwithstanding Carey's criticisms, and as we said in chapter 3, commentators in general seem agreed that any organisation has two major functions that are inseparable from one another, namely the *task function* and the *social function*; in a school these would be the *academic function* of teaching/learning and the *social function* of creating and distributing human satisfactions among teachers and pupils alike. Unlike the industrial model, where task efficiency (as measured, for example, by levels of productivity) can be linked to social satisfactions and social happiness, in the school the link is less clear. The only task efficiency or 'productivity' index is test or examination results which, as we have seen earlier, have limitations, though often used as the only measure available. As Edwards (1974) notes about school 'productivity':

In schools, better-than-average results may be produced by teachers and children who realise that they are responding to the special expectations communicated by a group of experimenters who are committed to the experiment and who would get an extra 'kick' out of special results. When the new methods are more widely adopted they may lose their special appeal and results may be little better or worse than those produced by earlier methods. However, this argument that change or novelty can of itself produce beneficial but perhaps shortlived and non-generalisable results should not be taken as an argument that all advocated changes are equally unlikely to produce widespread and long-term advantages. What it might lead us to consider is that each teacher should find his own ways of making his pupils feel they are 'special', but this, of course, might always have been one of the secrets of the good teacher.

INTERPERSONAL EXPECTATION AND THE SELF-FULFILLING PROPHECY

Interpersonal expectation The expectation held by one individual concerning the behaviour of another individual or group of individuals, is a powerful influence on behavioural change — as the Hawthorne studies showed. Even outside the group context it can operate. For example, Frank (1963) talks about the 'Hallo–Goodbye' effect in psychotherapy. Patients who merely had contact with a prestigious medical practitioner showed statistically significant improvement over waiting-list patients who were not seen, but who were used as a 'control group', and almost as much improvement as those who received prolonged therapy. (There is no record of the 'Goodbye–Hallo' effect, that is where contact, however brief, with a prestigious 'anti-medicine' man might result in deterioration, though I suspect the phenomenon could work in reverse in much the same way.)

Interpersonal expectations give rise to the *self-fulfilling prophecy*. Essentially the *self-fulfilling prophecy* is, in the beginning, a false definition of the situation between two persons (or one person and a group) that evokes from the recipient of the definition a new behaviour that makes the originally false conception come true. Some such prophecies Johnson (1970) calls *benign*, others he calls *malignant*. An example of the *benign* would be where a child's expectations that his new school fellows would be friendly can help considerably to create friendly peer-group relations; of the *malignant* when a child is falsely defined as being of inferior ability which helps to create expectations that lead to him being labelled as inferior. Johnson suggests that the problem is for the teacher to support benign prophecies and intervene in ways that terminate malignant prophecies. One index of a skilled and successful teacher might be the teacher who can make his prophecies come true, and Edwards touches on the same question in the above passage.

EDUCATIONAL IMPLICATIONS OF THE HAW-THORNE EXPERIMENT

The Hawthorne experiment was very important in my view, not only because it became almost a benign form of the self-fulfilling prophecy, but because of its effect on experiments in the social sciences in general, and education in particular, an effect that has still not been fully recognised.

We spoke earlier about the need for attention that acts as a powerful motivating force on human behaviour. This is what the workers, especially the selected female group, received in the Hawthorne experiment. Essentially, the consideration accorded to them resulted in higher output because *it met more of their psychological and social needs than was normally the case.* The same conditions often obtain in educational circumstances, for example, in the case of educationally retarded children. Research programmes undertaken with them can result in big gains in measured attainment while the programme is actively in operation, but this level falls away when the programme is over, perhaps eventually falling to levels virtually indistinguishable from those attained by children who were not engaged in the original programme at all.

The key problem, then, of the educational process is how the Hawthorne effect of 'special involvement' might be continued right through a child's career in school so that he realises his capabilities and potential to the full. Realistically we know that this is unlikely to happen on any large scale since teachers, whatever their abilities, are generally unable to make each child's case 'special'. For the social context in which teachers work will always be an uneven one, as is the social context of society generally. Hence it will be a matter of luck or chance whether teacher and child can *together* provide the appropriate learning environment (I say 'together' since both parties have responsibilities in the matter, even given that the teacher's element may be the larger). What might be said with reasonable certainty is that an awareness of the social context in which a teacher works should enable him the more easily to come to terms with the extensive demands that teaching makes upon him.

Further reading

GENERAL READING

ARGYLE, M. (1972) *The Psychology of Interpersonal Behaviour*, 2nd ed. (Harmondsworth: Penguin)

HARGREAVES, D. H. (1972) *Interpersonal Relations and Education* (London: Routledge and Kegan Paul)

MORRISON, A. and MCINTYRE, D. (1973) *Teachers and Teaching*, 2nd ed. (Harmondsworth: Penguin)

CHAPTER 1. INTERACTION IN CLASSROOM GROUPS

ARGYLE, M. (1969) *Social interaction* (London: Methuen)

CARTWRIGHT, D. and ZANDER, A. (1969) *Group Dynamics*, 3rd ed. (London: Tavistock)

GAHAGAN, J. (1975) *Interpersonal and Group Behaviour* (London: Methuen)

SMITH, P. B. (1970) *Group Processes* (Harmondsworth: Penguin)

CHAPTER 2. PERSON PERCEPTION AND CLASS-ROOM COMMUNICATION

CICOUREL, A. V. (1972) *Cognitive Sociology* (Harmondsworth: Penguin)

GIGLIOLI, P. P. (1972) (ed.) *Language and Social Context* (Harmondsworth: Penguin)

HASTORF, A., SCHNEIDER, D. and POLFKA, J. (1970) *Person Perception* (Reading, Mass.: Addison-Wesley)

SMITH, H. C. (1968) 'Sensitivity to People', in H. Toch and H. C. Smith (eds), *Social Perception* (Princeton: Van Nostrand)

CHAPTER 3. LEADERSHIP IN TEACHING

FIEDLER, F. E. (1971) 'Validation and Extension of the Contingency

Model of Leadership Effectiveness; A Review of Empirical Findings', *Psychological Bulletin* **76**, 128-48

FLEISHMAN, E. A., and HUNT, J. G. (1973) (eds) *Current Developments in the Study of Leadership* (Carbondale, Ill.: Illinois University Press)

GIBB, C. A. (1969) (ed.) *Leadership* (Harmondsworth: Penguin)

RICHARDSON, E. (1973) *The Teacher, the School and the Task of Management* (London: Heinemann Educational)

CHAPTER 4. COMMUNICATION, SOCIAL LEARNING AND CONTROL IN TEACHING

BANDURA, A. (1970) *Principles of Behavior Modification* (New York: Holt, Rinehart and Winston)

MCLEISH, J., MATHESON, W., and PARK, J. (1973) *The Psychology of the Learning Group* (London: Hutchinson)

MORRISON, A. and MCINTYRE, D. (1971) *Schools and Socialization* (Harmondsworth: Penguin)

WHELDALL, K. (1975) *Social Behaviour* (London: Methuen)

CHAPTER 5. TEACHER BEHAVIOUR IN ORGANISATIONAL SETTINGS

ARGYLE, M. (1974) *The Social Psychology of Work* (Harmondsworth: Penguin)

JOHNSON, D. W. (1970) *The Social Psychology of Education* (New York: Holt, Rinehart and Winston)

KORMAN, A. K. (1971) *Industrial and Organisational Psychology* (Englewood Cliffs, N.J.: Prentice-Hall)

WARR, P. and WALL, T. (1975) *Work and Well-Being* (Harmondsworth: Penguin)

References and Name index

The numbers in italics following each entry are page references to discussions of authors within this book.

ARGYLE, M. (1972) *The Psychology of Interpersonal Behaviour*, 2nd ed. (Harmondsworth: Penguin). *27, 42, 45, 97*

ARGYLE, M. (1974) *The Social Psychology of Work* (Harmondsworth: Penguin). *143, 145*

ARGYLE, M. (1975) *Bodily Communication* (London: Methuen). *44, 47*

ASCH, S. A. (1956) 'Studies of Independence and Conformity. A Minority of One Against a Unanimous Majority', *Psychological Monograph* **70** No. 9. *35, 144*

BALES, R. F. (1950) *Interaction Process Analysis* (Cambridge, Mass.: Addison-Wesley). *21*

BALES, R. F. (1958) 'Task Roles and Social Roles in Problem Solving Groups', in E. Maccoby, T. M. Newcomb and E. L. Hartley (eds), *Readings in Social Psychology*, 3rd ed. (New York: Holt, Rinehart and Winston). *76*

BANDURA, A. (1971) *Social Learning Theory* (New York: General Learning Press). *103*

BANDURA, A. and KUPERS, C. J. (1964) 'The Transmission of Patterns of Self-Reinforcement through Modeling', *Journal of Abnormal and Social Psychology* **69**, 1-9. *110*

BANDURA, A. and WALTERS, R. H. (1963) *Social Learning and Personality Development* (New York: Holt, Rinehart and Winston). *103, 109*

BAUER, R. A. (1964) 'The Obstinate Audience: The Influence Process From the Point of View of Social Communication', *American Psychologist* **19**, 319-28. *93*

BERNSTEIN, B. (1961) 'Social Structure, Language and learning', *Educational Research* **3**, 163-76. *45*

BERNSTEIN, B. (1971) *Class, Codes and Control* (London: Routledge and Kegan Paul), vol. 1. *45*

BIDWELL, C. E. (1965) 'The School as Formal Organisation', in J. G.

March (ed.), *Handbook of organisations* (Skokie, Ill.: Rand McNally). *130*

BLUM, J. P. and GUMPERZ, J. (1971) 'Some Social Determinants of Verbal Behaviour', in J. Gumperz and D. Hymes (eds), *Directions in Sociolinguistics* (New York: Holt, Rinehart and Winston). *63*

BRONFENBRENNER, V., HARDING, J., and GALLWAY, M. (1958) 'The Measurement of Skill in Social Perception', in D. C. McClelland, A. L. Baldwin, V. Bronfenbrenner and F. L. Strodtbeck (eds), *Talent and Society* (Princeton: Van Nostrand). *55*

BROWN, G. (1977) *Child Development* (London: Open Books). *104*

BROWN, R. (1965) *Social Psychology* (London: Collier-Macmillan). *52*

CALDER, N. (1976) *The Human Conspiracy* (London: BBC Publications). *ix*

CAREY, A. (1967) 'The Hawthorne Studies: A Radical Criticism', *American Sociological Review* 32, 403-16. *154*

CARLSON, R. O. (1965) 'Barriers to Change in Public Schools', in R. O. Carlson, A. Gallaher, Jr, M. B. Miles, R. J. Pellegrin and E. M. Robers, *Change Processes in the Public Schools* (Eugene, Oregon: Center for Advanced Study in Educational Administration). *142*

CARTWRIGHT, D. and ZANDER, A. (1969) *Group Dynamics*, 3rd ed. (London: Tavistock). *9, 10, 21*

CHOMSKY, N. (1959) 'Review of Skinner's *Verbal Behaviour*', *Language* 35, 26-58. *104, 111*

CHOMSKY, N. (1965) *Aspects of a Theory of Syntax* (Cambridge, Mass.: MIT Press). *62*

CICOUREL, A. V. (1973) *Cognitive Sociology* (Harmondsworth: Penguin). *63*

CLINE, V. B. and RICHARDS, J. M., Jr (1960) 'Accuracy of Interpersonal Perception — a General Trait?', *Journal of Abnormal and Social Psychology* 60, 1-7. *54*

COLEMAN, J. S. (1961) *The Adolescent Society* (New York: Free Press). *117*

CONNOR, D. V. (1960) 'Behaviour in Class Groups on Contrasting Climate', *British Journal of Educational Psychology* 30, 244-9. *149*

COOPER, J. B., and MCGAUGH, J. L. (1963) *Integrating Principles of Social Psychology* (New York: Schankman). *70*

CORTIS, G. A. (1973) 'The Relationship of Sociology and Psychology in an Educational Context: A Psychologist's Viewpoint', *Educational Review* 25, 250-62. *10, 130*

DAVIS, J. H. (1969) *Group Performance* (Reading, Mass.: Addison-Wesley). *16, 25*

DAVISON, W. P. (1959) 'On the Effects of Communication', *Public Opinion Quarterly* 23, 343-60. *93*

EDWARDS, W. T. (1974) *Social Psychology: Theories and Discussions*

(London: Longman). *154*

FESHBACK, S. and SINGER, R. D. (1957) 'The Effects of Fear Arousal and Suppression of Fear upon Social Perception', *Journal of Abnormal and Social Psychology* **55**, 283-8. *51*

FESTINGER, L. (1957) *A Theory of Cognitive Dissonance* (New York: Harper and Row). *115, 140*

FIEDLER, F. (1960) 'The Leader's Psychological Distance and Group Effectiveness', in D. Cartwright and A. Zander, *Group Dynamics*, 2nd ed. (New York: Harper and Row). *81*

FINLAYSON, D. (1975) 'Organisational Climate', *Research Intelligence* **1**, 22-36. *151*

FLANDERS, N. A. (1967) 'Teacher Influence in the Classroom', in E. J. Amidon and J. B. Hough *Interaction Analysis: Theory Research and Application* (Reading, Mass.: Addison-Wesley). *79*

FLANDERS, N. A. (1970) *Analysing Teacher Behaviours* (Reading, Mass.: Addison-Wesley). *79*

FLEISHMAN, E. A. (1973) 'Twenty Years of Consideration and Structures', in E. A. Fleishman and J. G. Hunt (eds), *Current Developments in the Study of Leadership* (Carbondale, Ill.: Southern Illinois University Press). *80*

FONTANA, D. (1977) *Personality and Education* (London: Open Books). *140, 142*

FRANK, J. D. (1963) *Persuasion and Healing* (New York: Schocken Books). *155*

GETZELS, J. W. and GUBA, E. G. (1957) 'Social Behaviour and the Administrative Process', *School Review* **65**, 423-41. *80*

GETZELS, J. W. and THELEN, H. A. (1960) 'The Classroom as a Unique Social System', in N. B. Henry (ed.), *The Dynamics of instructional Groups*, The 59th Year Book of the National Society for the Study of Education, Part 2 (University of Chicago Press). *3*

GIBB, C. A. (1954) 'Leadership', in G. Lindzey (ed.), *Handbook of Social Psychology* (Cambridge, Mass.: Addison-Wesley). *73*

GIBB, C. A. (1969) (ed.) *Leadership* (Harmondsworth: Penguin). *77*

GIGLIOLI, P. P. (1972) (ed.) *Language and Social Context* (Harmondsworth: Penguin). *62*

GOFFMAN, E. (1964) 'The Neglected Situation', *American Anthropologist* **66**, 133-6. *58*

GOFFMAN, E. (1968) *Asylums* (Harmondsworth: Penguin). *137*

GOLDBERG, M. H. and MACCOBY, E. E. (1965) 'Children's Acquisition of Skill in Performing a Group Task under Two Conditions of Group Formation', *Journal of Personality and Social Psychology* **2**, 898-902. *118*

GOLEMBIEWSKI, R. T. (1962) *The Small Group* (University of Chicago Press). *1*

GURIN, G., VEROFF, J., and FELD, S. (1960) *Americans View their Mental Health* (New York: Basic Books). *135*

GUTHRIE, E. R. (1952) *The Psychology of Learning* (New York: Harper). *95*

HALPIN, A. W. and CROFT, D. B. (1973) *The Organisational Climate of Schools* (Chicago University: Mid-West Administrative Center). *151*

HARARY, F., NORMAN, R. Z., and CARTWRIGHT, Z. (1965) *Structural Models* (New York: Wiley). *25*

HARGREAVES, D. H. (1967) *Social Relations in a Secondary School* (London: Routledge and Kegan Paul). *101, 147*

HARGREAVES, D. H. (1972) *Interpersonal Relations and Education* (London: Routledge and Kegan Paul). *138, 144*

HARVEY, O. J., PRATHER, M., WHITE, B. J., and HOFFMEISTER, J. (1968) 'Teachers' Beliefs, Classroom Atmosphere and Student Behaviour', *American Educational Research Journal* **5**, 151-65. *149*

HAVIGHURST, R. J. (1953) *Human Development and Education* (New York: Longmans). *65*

HERZBERG, F. (1966) *Work and the Nature of Man* (New York: World Publishing Company). *133*

HERZBERG, F., MAUSNER, B., and SNYDERMAN, G. (1959) *The Motivation to Work* (New York: Wiley). *133*

HOFFER, E. (1951) *The True Believer* (New York: Harper). *91*

HOLLANDER, E. P. (1964) (ed.) *Leaders, Groups and Influence* (New York: Oxford University Press). *73. 101*

HOLLANDER, E. P. and JULIAN, J. W. (1968) 'Leadership', in E. F. Borgatta and W. W. Lambert (eds), *Handbook of Personality Theory and Research* (Chicago: Rand McNally). *91*

HOMANS, G. C. (1950) *The Human Group* (New York: Harcourt, Brace and World). *21*

INGLEBY, D. (1974) 'The Psychology of Child Psychology', in M. P. M. Richards (ed.), *The Integration of a Child into a Social World* (Cambridge University Press). *21*

JACKSON, P. W. (1968) *Life in Classrooms* (New York: Holt, Rinehart and Winston). *55*

JOHNSON, D. W. (1970) *The Social Psychology of Education* (New York: Holt, Rinehart and Winston). *155*

KAHN, R. L. and KATZ, D. (1960) 'Leadership Practices in Relation to Productivity and Morale', in D. Cartwright and A. Zander, *Group Dynamics*, 2nd ed. (New York: Harper and Row). *77*

KAHN, R. L., WOLFE, D., QUINN, R., SNOEK, J., and ROSENTHAL, R. (1964) *Organisational Stress: Studies in Role Conflict and Ambiguity* (New York: Wiley). *130*

KATZ, D. and KAHN, R. L. (1966) *The Social Psychology of*

Organisations (New York: Wiley). *129, 130, 131*

KELVIN, P. (1969) *The Bases of Social Behaviour* (London: Holt, Rinehart and Winston). *28*

KING, N. (1970) 'Classification and Evaluation of the Two-Factor Theory of Job Satisfaction', *Psychological Bulletin* **74**, 18-31. *134*

KOUNIN, J. S. and GUMP, P. V. (1958) 'The Ripple Effect in Discipline', *Elementary School Journal* **59**, 158-62. *126*

KUHN, M. H. (1964) 'The Reference Group Reconsidered, *Sociological Quarterly* **5**, 6-21. *104*

LEACH, D. J. and RAYBOULD, E. C. (1977) *Learning and Behaviour Difficulties in School* (London: Open Books). *94*

LEWIN, K., LIPPITT, R., and WHITE, R. (1939) 'Patterns of Aggressive Behaviour in Experimentally Created Social Climates', *Journal of Social Psychology* **10**, 271-99. *90, 148*

LIKERT, R. (1967) *The Human Organisation: Its Management and Value* (New York: McGraw-Hill). *130*

LINDGREN, H. C. (1969) *An Introduction to Social Psychology* (New York: Wiley). *89, 98*

LINDZEY, G. and BRYNE, D. (1968) 'Measurement of Social Choice and Interpersonal Attractiveness', in G. Lindzey and E. Aronson (eds), *The Handbook of Social Psychology* (Reading, Mass.: Addison-Wesley), vol. 2. *25*

LOWIN, A. and CRAIG, J. R. (1968) 'The Influence of Level of Performance on Managerial Style: An Experimental Object-Lesson in the Ambiguity of Correlational Data', *Organisational Behaviour and Human Performance* **3**, 440-58. *72*

MACCOBY, N., JECKER, J., BREITROSE, H. S., and ROSE, E. D. (1964) 'Sound Film Recordings in Improving Classroom Communications', in *Experimental Studies in Classroom Communication* (Stanford: Institute for Communication Research). *96*

MACCOBY, N., and MARKLE, D. G. (1973) 'Communication and Learning', in S. Schramm, I. Pool, N. Maccoby, E. B. Parker and F. W. Frey (eds), *Handbook of Communication* (Chicago: Rand McNally). *96*

MCGREGOR, D. (1960) *The Human Side of Enterprise* (New York: McGraw-Hill). *141*

MCGREGOR, D. (1966) *Leadership and Motivation* (Cambridge, Mass.: MIT Press). *141*

MCLEISH, J. (1976) 'Learning in Groups: Facilitation and Inhibition Processes', *Bulletin of the British Psychological Society* **29**, 7-15. *95, 111, 112*

MCLEISH, J., MATHESON, W., and PARK, J. (1973) *The Psychology of the Learning Group* (London: Hutchinson). *111*

MADSEN, C. H., BECKER, W. C., and THOMAS, D. R. (1968) 'Rules,

Praise and Ignoring: Elements of Elementary Classroom Control', *Journal of Applied Behavioral Analysis* **1**, 139-50. *123*

MARCH, J. G. and SIMON, H. A. (1958) *Organisations* (New York: Wiley). *11*

MASLOW, A. H. (1943) 'A Theory of Human Motivation', *Psychological Review* **50**, 370-96. *132*

MILLER, G. A. (1965) 'Some Preliminaries to Psycholinguistics', *American Psychologist* **20**, 15-20. *104*

MILLER, N. E. and DOLLARD, J. (1941) *Social Learning and Imitation* (New Haven, Conn.: Yale University Press). *95*

MINTZ, A. (1951) 'Non-Adaptive Group Behavior', *Journal of Abnormal and Social Psychology* **46**, 150-9. *118*

MORENO, J. L. (1953) *Who Shall Survive?* (New York: Beacon House). *21, 148*

MORRISON, A. and McINTYRE, D. (1973) *Teachers and Teaching*, 2nd ed. (Harmondsworth: Penguin). *12, 69*

MUSGROVE, F. and TAYLOR, P. H. (1969) *Society and the Teacher's Role* (London: Routledge and Kegan Paul). *122*

NELSON, P. D. (1964) 'Similarities and Differences Among Leaders and Followers', *Journal of Social Psychology* **63**, 161-7. *74*

NEWCOMB, T. M. (1961) *The Acquaintance Process* (New York: Holt, Rinehart and Winston). *13*

NEWCOMB, T. M., TURNER, R. H. and CONVERSE, P. E. (1965) *Social Psychology* (New York: Holt, Rinehart and Winston). *28, 49, 81, 86*

NORTHWAY, M. L. and WELD, L. (1967) *Sociometric Testing* (University of Toronto Press). *22*

PAGE, E. B. (1958) 'Teacher Comments and Student Performance: A Seventy-Four Classroom Experiment in Social Motivation', *Journal of Educational Psychology*, **49**, 173-81. *107*

RICHARDSON, E. (1967) *The Environment of Learning* (London: Nelson). *47*

RIDING, R. (1977) *School Learning, Mechanisms and Processes* (London: Open Books). *94*

ROETHLISBERGER, F. J. and DICKSON, W. J. (1964) *Management and the Worker* (Cambridge, Mass.: Harvard University Press). *153*

SECORD, P. F. and BACKMAN, C. W. (1964) *Social Psychology* (New York: McGraw-Hill). *38*

SHEFFIELD, F. D. (1961) 'Theoretical Consideration in the Learning of Complex Sequential Tasks from Demonstration and Practice', in A. A. Lumsdaine (ed.), *Student Response in Programmed Instruction: A Symposium* (Washington, D.C.: National Academy of Sciences). *95*

SHERIF, M. (1936) *The Psychology of Social Norms* (New York:

Harper). *32, 33, 144*

SHERIF, M. (1963) 'Social Psychology: Problems and Trends in Interdisciplinary Relationships', in S. Koch (ed.), *Psychology, a Study of a Science*, vol. 6: *Investigations of Man as a Socius* (New York: McGraw-Hill). *113*

SHERIF, M. and SHERIF, C. (1953) *Groups in Harmony and Tension* (New York: Harper and Row). *16*

SKINNER, B. F. (1953) *Science and Human Behavior* (New York: McMillan). *94*

SKINNER, B. F. (1957) *Verbal Behavior* (New York: Appleton-Century-Crofts). *104, 111*

SKINNER, B. F. (1963) 'Operant Behavior', *American Psychologist* **18**, 503-15. *106*

SKINNER, B. F. (1969) *Contingencies of Reinforcement: A Theoretical Analysis* (New York: Appleton-Century-Crofts). *94*

SMITH, H. C. (1968) 'Sensitivity to People', in H. Toch and H. C. Smith (eds), *Social Perception* (Princeton, N.J.: Van Nostrand). *56*

STAUB, E. (1971) 'A Child in Distress: The Influence of Nurturance and Modeling on Children's Attempts to Help', *Developmental Psychology* **5**, 124-32. *105*

STEVENSON, H. W. and HILL, H. J. (1966) 'Use of Rate as a Measure of Response in Studies of Social Reinforcement', *Psychological Bulletin* **66**, 321-6. *107*

STOGDILL, R. M. (1948) 'Personal Factors Associated with Leadership: A Survey of the Literature', *Journal of Psychology* **25**, 35-71. *68*

SULLIVAN, H. S. (1940) *Conceptions of Modern Psychiatry* (New York: White Psychiatric Foundation). *104*

TAGUIRI, R. and LITWIN, G. H. (1968) *Organisational Climate: Exploration of a Concept* (Cambridge, Mass.: Harvard Business School). *146*

THELEN, H. A. (1960) 'Exploration of a Growth Model for Psychic, Biological and Social Systems', unpublished paper cited in Katz and Kahn (1966). *99*

THIBAUT, J. W. and KELLEY, H. H. (1959) *The Social Psychology of Groups* (New York: Wiley). *28*

TUDDENHAM, R. D. and MCBRIDE, P. D. (1959) 'The Yielding Experiment from the Subject's Point of View', *Journal of Personality* **27**, 259-71. *114*

VENESS, T. (1962) 'Small Social Groups', in G. Humphrey and M. Argyle (eds), *Social Psychology through Experiment* (London: Methuen). *13*

VROOM, V. H. (1964) *Work and Motivation* (New York: Wiley). *134*

WALL, T. D., STEPHENSON, G. M., and SKIDMORE, C. (1971) 'Ego Involvement and Herzberg's Two-Factor Theory of Job Satisfaction: An Experimental Field Study', *British Journal of Social and Clinical Psychology*, **10**, 123-31. *134*

WALLER, W. (1965) *The Sociology of Teaching* (first published 1932) (New York: Wiley). *92, 140*

WARR, P. B. and WALL, T. (1975) *Work and Well-Being* (Harmondsworth: Penguin). *72*

WATSON, G. (1966) *Social Psychology: Issues and Insights* (New York: J. B. Lippincott). *142*

WEBER, M. (1947) *The Theory of Social and Economic Organisation* (New York: Free Press). *91, 129*

WHELDALL, K. (1975) *Social Behaviour* (London: Methuen). *121*

WILSON, B. (1962) 'The Teacher's Role — a Sociological Analysis', *British Journal of Sociology* **13**, 15-32. *137, 146*

WITHALL, J. (1951) 'The Development of a Climate Index', *Journal of Educational Research* **45**, 93-100. *149*

WOLF, M. G. (1970) 'Need Gratification Theory: A Theoretical Reformation of Job Satisfaction/Dissatisfaction and Job Motivation', *Journal of Applied Psychology* **54**, 89-94. *132*

Subject index